THE
MOUNTAINS
OF ISRAEL

THE MOUNTAINS OF ISRAEL

The Bible & the West Bank

by Norma Parrish Archbold
Illustrated by Marita Brokenshaw

שירת פיבי

Phoebe's Song - Israel and USA

Cover design by the author
Cover illustration by Marita Brokenshaw
Illustrations from historical photos

English Editions
Printed in Jerusalem, USA, Australia
First Edition - Printed 1993
Second Edition - Printed 1993, 1994, 1996, 1998, 1999, 2001
Third Edition 1994
Fourth Edition 1996, 1999, 2001

Norwegian Edition
Printed in Norway
First Edition - Printed 1993, 1995, 1999, 2001

Telegu (India) Edition
Printed in India
First Edition - Printed 1993, 1995, 1997, 1999, 2001

Spanish Edition
Printed in Guatemala
First Edition - Printed in 1997, 1999

Bulgarian Edition
Printed in Bulgaria
First Edition - 1997, 1999

The Mountains of Israel...The Bible & the West Bank,
Copyright ©1993, 1994, 1995, 1996 by Norma Parrish
Archbold. All rights reserved.

FOURTH EDITION

U.S.$9.95/Canada $12.75/Israel NIS 30.00
ISBN 965-90100-0-1

In gratitude to the LORD...
the God of Abraham, Isaac and Jacob...
for His love and His mercy.

CONTENTS

Maps

Illustrations By Marita Brokenshaw

Other Illustrations

FOREWORD

A profound ignorance exists today concerning what is taking place in the land of Israel. If you believe the picture presented by the media, the Palestinians are cruelly oppressed and denied possession of their native land, which was stolen from them by an invading Israeli army. Those who subscribe to this view, however, either don't know (or don't want to acknowledge) the true history and significance of the current situation.

What is the West Bank and why have the Israelis held onto it so fiercely? Why not give it to the Palestinians, if it would mean peace? What is Israel's claim to the land, and is it greater than the Palestinians' claim? The answers to these questions are of vital importance to an understanding of Middle Eastern events, yet too few people know, or even care to find out, the underlying issues that are driving the Israeli/Palestinian conflict and the ongoing "peace" negotiations.

That is why I am glad to recommend Norma Archbold's *The Mountains of Israel*. Archbold has a deep and abiding love for Israel, both the land and the people, and has appeared on my national TV program, *Zola Levitt Presents*. Her timely study addresses many of the issues that are being ignored by today's scholars and media commentators. She presents clearly and concisely the history behind Israel's claim to the land, documenting with Scripture its indisputable right of possession, and using maps, charts and drawings to clearly show Israel past and present, as well as the current areas of land in dispute.

Israel is not just another small parcel of land over in the Middle East somewhere. It has had a profound impact on history and will have a predominant role in the future. It first came into being 3,500 years ago when God told Abraham, "unto thy seed have I given this land" (Genesis 15:18). This was the first of many promises concerning the land, and laid the foundation for Israel's restoration as modern-day Jewish nation. God's promise to Abraham was unconditional, eternal and specific. The people of Israel are a people of destiny. We are seeing today the fulfillment of Isaiah 34:17- 35:1,

"They shall possess it forever, from generation to generation shall they dwell therein. The wilderness and the solitary place shall be glad for them; and the desert shall rejoice, and blossom as the rose."

But the sovereignty of Israel is being threatened. The Israeli government is being pressured to give away the land promised by God to Abraham's descendants, specifically the area know as the West Bank. This misleading name has been popularized by the media and refers to the time when this portion of the land was annexed by the country of Jordan, thereby forming its "West Bank." This area is actually the part of ancient Israel known as Judea and Samaria, and contains most of Israel's mountains. As Archbold put it, "The mountains of Israel are the heart of the Land promised by God to the children of Israel." The enemies of the Chosen People are trying to bleed this away. The "peace" process is ultimately intended to lead to the destruction of Israel as a nation.

Those who believe in the Scriptures have a responsibility to stand against this and support Israel. The first step is to understand what is happening so that we can counter the lies and misinformation, and this is one reason that Archbold's study is so important. I would encourage every believer to read this book. After all, this is the land where we will live for a 1,000 years with our King. It is in our best interest to give it all the assistance we can.

Zola Levitt
Zola Levitt Presents

FOREWORD

As a college freshman in the late 70's, beginning to grapple with the issues in the Middle East, I pictured the "West Bank" as a sandy strip of land about a kilometer wide flanking the Jordan River. It was hard to fathom why those obstinate Israelis would insist on blocking peace by holding on to such an insignificant piece of real estate, and furthermore, why they would provoke the Arab population there by erecting Jewish settlements.

Fifteen years later, nine of which I have spent in Israel, I find myself residing in one of those "settlements", in the heart of Biblical Samaria, approximately equidistant between the Mediterranean Sea and Israel's border with Jordan. It has been a long odyssey for me—intellectually and spiritually—to come to understand the Lord's plans and purposes for the ingathering of the Jewish people to this little piece of land, of which Judea and Samaria, are an integral part.

I wish that fifteen years ago I had had access to the material presented in Norma Archbold's, *The Mountains of Israel*. In it, God's purposes for the land of Israel, and in particular, the hill country of Judea and Samaria, as outlined in the Biblical prophets, are clearly and concisely presented.

The layman wanting to be informed on current issues, but having neither the time nor the inclination for lengthy scholarly works on the subject, will find this book a thought-provoking "quick-read". The Biblical passages and modern day fulfillments are juxtapositioned. The sources are documented for those interested in further research.

In many instances, the author adds few comments, as the Biblical passages she presents speak clearly for themselves. The Sovereign Lord says to the mountains of Israel:

"I will cause you to be inhabited as you were formerly . . . I will cause men—my people Israel— to walk on you and possess you, so that you will become their inheritance . . . ."

(Ezekiel 36:11,12 NASB).

The Mountains of Israel is a book I can enthusiastically recommend to all those who have a respect for the Hebrew scriptures and wish to know what light they shed upon the present situation in the Middle East. Even those dubious about the relevance of the Bible to current issues will find evidence here that will challenge them to reconsider their views.

With the "West Bank" and Israeli-Arab peace negotiations daily in the news, this a subject on which each one of us wants to be informed. *The Mountains of Israel* is an excellent source with which to begin.

Sheila Gyllenberg
MA Jewish History
Bar Ilan University, Israel

INTRODUCTION

For everyone who loves the Lord, the God of Abraham, Isaac and Jacob, the events unfolding in the Middle East are important.

It is difficult, however, to form a clear picture of what is happening. The news in the West about the Arab-Israeli conflict is incomplete and often inaccurate and is interpreted by people, who do not necessarily believe in the Bible, or have a clear overall picture of the 4,000-year-old conflict.

Without an overall picture of the conflict the events mentioned in the news are meaningless. Years of historical research is necessary to find the missing pieces. To match history with the Word of God one must also be a serious student of the Bible.

For many people understanding the Arab-Israeli conflict is so difficult that they have given up.

In studying the Middle East conflict I was struck by the similarity of Middle East events and chapters 35 and 36 of Ezekiel.

These chapters are two halves of a whole. Chapter 35 is a prophecy "against" a mountain (Mount Seir) and chapter 36 is a prophecy "to" mountains (the mountains of Israel). Mount Seir and the mountains of Israel are the homelands of twin brothers Esau and Jacob, ancestors of today's Arabs and Jews.

Introduction

Although chapter 35 contains warnings and chapter 36 contains promises, the purpose is the same. Both chapters end with the same words, "Then they shall know that I am the Lord."

By revealing the similarity between these chapters and historical and current events *The Mountains of Israel* provides a context for the bits and pieces we pick up in the news.

The Bible has much to say about the Arab-Israeli conflict. But without knowing the identity of Edom and the location of Mount Seir and of the mountains of Israel, one can read right past some startling information without understanding that it affects the Middle East, the world and important decisions being made today.

The Mountains of Israel provides these important missing pieces which point out the truth of the Bible, revealing God's great power, wisdom, and faithfulness.

This is not a chatty book. I use just enough words to help you to see the picture without getting lost in complicated side issues. Simple maps and other illustrations make a point with few words.

To help you feel the desolation of Israel before the return of the Jewish people, I have included quotes from eyewitnesses—Gentiles who traveled here in the 18th and 19th centuries. You will see that Israel was a treeless, barren wasteland.

The population a century and a half ago was less than 4% of today's population. As you read the eye witness reports imagine what Israel must have been like without 96% of its population.

In the last century those who visited the Holy Land testified of its condition. "A desolate country," "wretched desolation and neglect," "almost abandoned now," "unoccupied," "uninhabited," "thinly populated" is how they described the land.

The Reverend Samuel Manning said about the coastal plain, "This fertile plain, which might support an immense population, is almost a solitude...Day by day we were to learn afresh the lesson now forced upon us, that the denunciations of ancient prophecy have been fulfilled to the very letter—'the land is left void and desolate and without inhabitants.'"

Jews were among the sparse population—as prophesied more than 2,500 years ago.

"...the forsaken places are many in the...Land...but yet a tenth will be in it...as an oak whose stump remains when it is cut down so the holy seed shall be its stump." (Isaiah 6:12-13)

An official report in 1864 reveals that the largest group living in Jerusalem was Jewish.

God is keeping his promise to bring the children of Israel back to their land. Jewish people have been returning to Israel for more than 100 years. For a glimpse inside their hearts I have included the story of an Ethiopian girl, who walked through a desert, to fulfill her desire to be in Jerusalem.

What is happening today was foreseen and is working out according to the promises of God.

Introduction

When the Bible and the events in the Middle East are understood one cannot reasonably deny the existence of God. Properly understood, the events of today are earth shaking.

I took information from many sources and named them so you can study the subject as thoroughly as you wish. Bible references are given. The authority for this work rests firmly on the Bible— the Word of the Lord.

Those who do not accept God's Word will not accept the conclusions in *The Mountains of Israel*. But those who do accept the Bible as God's Word and who love Him, will find reason to rejoice. The Lord is keeping His promises in our day, proving that the Bible is true.

If you are one of the small group who have a good basic understanding of the Middle East situation, you already know how difficult it is to explain to others. *The Mountains of Israel* can give your family and friends the overview they need to understand the issues. Teachers and others who speak about the Arab-Israeli situation will find this book helpful. You may want to use it as a text.

The Mountains of Israel should be equally helpful to both Christians and Jews. While it will be obvious to most readers that I am a believer in Jesus the Messiah, if you are Jewish, the facts presented here should interest you very much. After all, God is keeping His ancient promises to your people.

INTRODUCTION TO THE FOURTH EDITION

In spite of dramatic changes in Israel *(The Oslo Accord, the Cairo Agreement, increased terror in Israel and around the world, the death of Prime Minister Rabin and a new Israeli government)* no substantial changes were necessary because *The Mountains of Israel* is presented from a Biblical point of view. God's Word and His plan remains the same.

The major change was a population chart for 1882 and 1995 to better illustrate the barrenness of Israel before the return of the Jews.

I give glory to the Lord for this work. May it be a blessing to you.

N P Archbold

Acknowledgments...

My greatest debt is to the Lord who gave me understanding of the 'West Bank' prophecies in Ezekiel and the desire and strength to persevere until the book was complete. He also sent others to help and encourage me.

I want to thank my family, friends in America and friends in Israel who made this book possible. The complete story of the writing of this book would require another book to tell.

Thank you dear friends. I am deeply grateful.

THE MOUNTAINS OF ISRAEL

"Son of man prophesy to the mountains of Israel and say...
'O mountains of Israel, hear the word of the Lord!'"
(Ezekiel 36:1)

The mountains of Israel is the heart of the Land promised by God to the children of Israel. It is Judea and Samaria, the inheritance of the tribes of Judah, Benjamin, and Joseph.

Bethel, Ai, Shilo, and Shechem—made famous by Abraham, Jacob and Joshua—are located in the mountains of Israel. Joshua and the bones of Joseph (Joshua 24:30, 32) were buried in this area.

Bethany—the home of Mary, Martha, and Lazarus; **Bethlehem**—the home of David and the birthplace of Jesus; **Hebron**—where Abraham, Sarah, Isaac, Rebekah, Leah, and Jacob are buried and,

Jerusalem—where the temple stood, where David and Solomon ruled, and where Jesus died and rose again are all located in the mountains of Israel.

It may surprise you to learn that the so-called West Bank includes all the places mentioned above. The West Bank and the mountains of Israel are nearly identical.

 The West Bank and the mountains of Israel are nearly identical.

1

THE MOUNTAINS OF ISRAEL

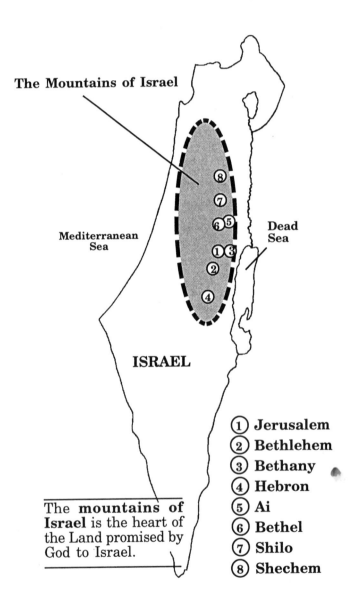

The Mountains of Israel

Mediterranean
Sea

Dead
Sea

ISRAEL

The **mountains of Israel** is the heart of the Land promised by God to Israel.

① Jerusalem
② Bethlehem
③ Bethany
④ Hebron
⑤ Ai
⑥ Bethel
⑦ Shilo
⑧ Shechem

2

'WEST BANK'
(Judea and Samaria)

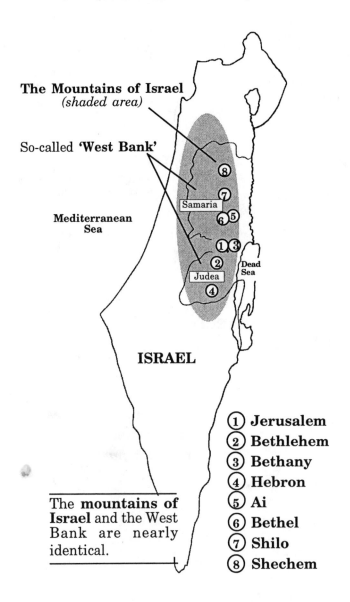

The **Mountains of Israel**
(shaded area)

So-called **'West Bank'**

Mediterranean
Sea

Samaria

Judea

Dead
Sea

ISRAEL

The **mountains of Israel** and the West Bank are nearly identical.

① Jerusalem
② Bethlehem
③ Bethany
④ Hebron
⑤ Ai
⑥ Bethel
⑦ Shilo
⑧ Shechem

ABRAHAM
IN THE MOUNTAINS OF ISRAEL

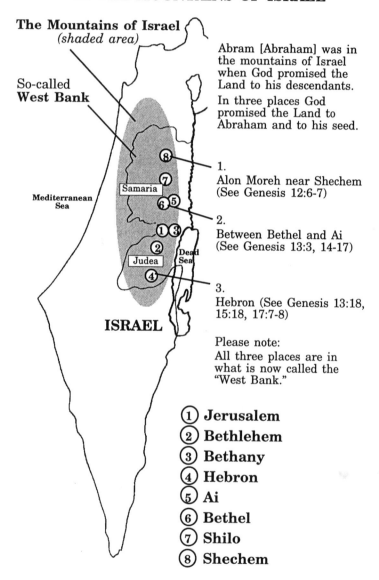

The Mountains of Israel
(shaded area)

So-called
West Bank

Mediterranean
Sea

Samaria

Judea

Dead
Sea

ISRAEL

Abram [Abraham] was in
the mountains of Israel
when God promised the
Land to his descendants.
In three places God
promised the Land to
Abraham and to his seed.

1.
Alon Moreh near Shechem
(See Genesis 12:6-7)

2.
Between Bethel and Ai
(See Genesis 13:3, 14-17)

3.
Hebron (See Genesis 13:18,
15:18, 17:7-8)

Please note:
All three places are in
what is now called the
"West Bank."

① **Jerusalem**
② **Bethlehem**
③ **Bethany**
④ **Hebron**
⑤ **Ai**
⑥ **Bethel**
⑦ **Shilo**
⑧ **Shechem**

THE PROMISE OF LAND

Abram (Abraham) was in in the mountains of Israel in the heart of the area sometimes referred to as the West Bank when the Lord promised him the Land *(see the map on page 4)*. The Lord said,

*"Arise, walk in the Land...for **I give it to you.**"*
(Genesis 13:17)

The boundaries of the Land promised to Abraham include all of modern day Israel, the disputed territories and much more. This promise was **un**conditional *(more about this later).*

*"...the LORD made a covenant with Abram, saying...'**To your descendants I have given this Land,** from the river of Egypt to the great river, the River Euphrates....'"*   *(Genesis 15:18)*

Abraham had seven sons in addition to Isaac *(Genesis 16:15; 25:1-2)*, but the covenant was established with Isaac.

Before the birth of Isaac, Abraham asked the Lord to give the promise to Ishmael,

"Oh, that Ishmael might live before You!"
(Genesis 17:18)

The Lord had other plans. He said to Abraham,

*"...No, Sarah your wife shall bear you a son, and you shall call his name Isaac; I will establish My covenant with him for an **everlasting covenant,** and with his descendants after him."*
(Genesis 17:19)

5

The promise passed from Isaac to Jacob and to Jacob's descendants, the Jewish people. Isaac gave Jacob this blessing,

*"May God Almighty bless you...and give the blessing of Abraham to you and your descendants with you **that you may inherit the Land**...which God gave to Abraham."* *(Genesis 28:3-4)*

The promise to Jacob was confirmed by God,

"I am the Lord God of Abraham your father and the God of Isaac; the Land on which you lie I will give to you and your descendants." *(Genesis 28:13)*

God promised the Land from the river of Egypt to the great River Euphrates *(Genesis 15:18, Joshua 1:4)* through Abraham and Isaac to Jacob and his descendants.

The Lord changed Jacob's name to Israel *(Genesis 35:10)*. Later in the Bible, Jacob's descendants were called in Hebrew 'B'nei Israel'—sons or children of Israel—or simply 'Israel'.

Jacob had 12 sons who established the tribes of Israel. The Lord brought the children of Israel out of Egypt to the Promised Land. Each Israeli tribe was given a portion of the Land *(see Joshua chapters 14-19)*.

The descendants of Judah *(a son of Jacob and Leah)* lived in the area called Judea, which includes Jerusalem, Hebron, Gaza, etc. *(see Joshua chapter 15)*.

Today the Children of Israel are called Jewish. The English word 'Jewish' comes from Judah. This would lead us to believe that only the descendants of Judah are Jewish. However, today in common English usage all the descendants of Jacob are Jewish. For example many people named Levin and Cohen are descendants of the Israeli tribe of Levi—not from Judah. But as language is used today, Levins and Cohens are Jewish.

The tribes of Israel are no longer separate. Intermarriage has formed Jacob's descendants into one group called the Jewish people or Israel. Today the names 'children of Israel' and 'Jewish people' are synonymous.

The Bible refers to the Children of Israel as Jewish in Ezra, Nehemiah, Esther, Jeremiah, Daniel, Zechariah and in 13 books of the New Testament.

(Note: Some point out that through the ages Gentiles, like Ruth the Moabite, converted to Judaism and became part of the Jewish people. Does this affect the identity of the group? No. Since those who convert marry within the Jewish community, their children are descendants of Jacob.)

A Dependable Promise

As stated above the promise of Land to Abraham's descendants is **UN**conditional. It is a promise between the LORD and Himself.

In Abraham's time when two people made a binding covenant, they cut animals in two and walked between the pieces. Both parties were bound by the agreement.

Abraham asked how he could know that he would inherit the Land,

"...How shall I know that I will inherit it?"
(Genesis 15:8)
The Lord said to Abraham,
"Bring Me a...heifer, a...goat and a...ram...."
(Genesis 15:9)

Abraham cut them in two and laid the halves opposite each other. But Abraham did not walk between the pieces. The Bible tells us that only the Lord moved between the pieces.

"...when the sun went down and it was dark...a smoking oven and a burning torch passed between (the) pieces." *(Genesis 15:17)*

Only God was bound by the covenant. The promise was guaranteed by the Lord. Nothing was required of Abraham.

Did the Lord change His mind when Israel sinned? No, He punished them and

"...scattered (them) among the nations...."
(Ezekiel 36:19)

Yet says the Lord,

"for all that, when (Israel is) in the land of their enemies, I will not cast them away...to utterly destroy them and break My covenant with them,

but...I will remember the covenant of their ances-
tors, whom I brought out of the land of Egypt...."
(Leviticus 26:44-45)

And after their punishment He will,

"...take you (Israel) from among the nations, gather
you out of all countries, and bring you into your
own land." *(Ezekiel 36:24)*

The Lord scattered the descendants of Jacob
among the nations **and** He promised to bring them
back to the Land.

The promise cannot be broken because,

"...the gifts and the calling of God are irrevocable."
(Romans 11:29)

To make sure that we understand this, God told
us the same thing several times in the Bible. He
said that His love for the Jewish people is as
dependable as the sun, moon and stars.

"Thus says the Lord,

who gives the sun for a light by day, the laws of
the moon and stars for a light by night, who stirs
up the sea, so that its waves roar, (The Lord of
hosts is His name):

'If those ordinances depart from before Me, says
the Lord, the seed of Israel also shall cease from
being a nation before Me forever.'

Thus says the Lord,

'If heaven above can be measured, and the foun-
dations of the earth searched out beneath, I will

9

also cast off all the seed of Israel for all that they have done, says the Lord.'"   (Jeremiah 31:35-37)

The Lord will keep His promise. Think of this...if God broke His promise to Israel, how could followers of Jesus be sure He would keep His promises to them?

Some Who Returned to Israel in the 19th Century

As prophesied in the Bible and recorded in history the Lord scattered the Jewish people among the nations, leaving a tiny remnant in the Land. Nearly 2,000 years later they began to return to the Land.

In 1948 Israel became a Jewish State. In the miraculous Six-Day war in 1967, Jews returned to Judea and Samaria—the heart of the Promised Land.

Believers in Jesus, who know God's promises, are encouraged when the Lord brings Jewish people back to the Land. His faithfulness to Israel proves that He exists and that His promises can be trusted.

The Lord is keeping his promise to the Jewish people,

"...I will GATHER you from the nations and bring you back from the countries where you have been SCATTERED, and I will give you back the land of Israel again." *(Ezekiel 11:17)*

THE LORD'S PLAN FOR HIS LAND

While the Lord has promised the Land to the Children of Israel as an inheritance, they are not free to give it or sell it to others permanently, because the Land belongs to the Lord. The Lord said,

*"The Land shall not be sold permanently, for **the Land is Mine**...."*   *(Leviticus 25:23)*

In the year of Jubilee (the 50th year), land was to be returned to the original owners. When land was sold, it could be held only until the Jubilee. *(See Leviticus 25:8-17).*

In Ezekiel the Lord reminded us that the Land is His. He called it **"My Land."** He said,

*"...I have spoken in My burning jealousy against the rest of the nations and against all Edom, who gave **MY LAND** to themselves as a possession...."*
(Ezekiel 36:5)

Traditionally the Lord's Land, which He set aside for His special purpose nearly 4,000 years ago, has been called the Holy Land. In chapter 36 of Ezekiel the Lord reveals His plan for the Holy Land. The Lord promised to resettle the Jewish people in the mountains of Israel. *(Keep in mind that the so-called West Bank and the mountains of Israel are nearly identical. When the Lord speaks of the mountains of Israel, He is referring to the so-called West Bank.)*

12

*"...**mountains of Israel,** you shall shoot forth your branches and yield your fruit to My people Israel, for they are about to come...*

*"I will multiply men upon you, **all the house of Israel, all of it;** and the cities shall be inhabited and the ruins rebuilt.*

"...I will make you inhabited as in former times, and do better for you than at your beginnings....

Return to Israel (Haifa Port...1949)

Jewish People from Morocco Arrive in Israel

*"...I will cause men to walk on you, **My people Israel; they shall take possession of you and you shall be their inheritance**...*

"...I do not do this for your sake, O house of Israel, but for My holy name's sake...I will sanctify My great name...and the nations shall know that I am the LORD...

*"For **I will** take you from among the nations, **gather you** out of all countries, and **bring you into your own Land**."*

(Ezekiel 36:8,10-12, 22-24)

The Lord's plan is to settle Jewish people in the mountains of Israel *(including the so-called West Bank)*. Israel shall possess the mountains of Israel. This is the Word of the Lord.

Settlements in the 'West Bank'

Although the Bible clearly states that Jews will settle in Judea and Samaria *(the West Bank)*, the media and the world proclaim that it is wrong for them to settle there.

Some believers who do not know the Word of the Lord concerning the mountains of Israel, or who do not know that the mountains of Israel and the so-called West Bank are almost identical, echo the false notion that it is wrong for Jews to settle in the disputed areas.

ISRAEL AFTER THE SIX-DAY WAR

* Areas won by Israel during the six-day war—1967

**Golan Heights

Lebanon
Syria

**So-called West Bank

Mountains of Israel
(shaded area)

Samaria

**Gaza
Strip

Judea

Dead
Sea

Mediterranean Sea

ISRAEL

Jordan

** Sinai

Egypt

Saudi
Arabia

Red Sea

To the mountains of Israel the Lord said,

"I will cause men to walk on you, my people Israel; they shall take possession of you...."
(Ezekiel 36:12)

God promised that Jewish people would live and restore the land in Samaria. He said,

"...You shall yet plant vines on the mountains of Samaria...." *(Jeremiah 31:5)*

This Word of the Lord has been *(and is being)* fulfilled in miraculous ways in our lifetime. Beyond question only God could have brought about the events that led to the formation of the Jewish State.

In 1948 after the destruction of six-million Jewish people in Europe, a tiny remnant formed a Jewish State in the Holy Land. They were attacked by six surrounding Arabic Islamic nations. Arabic forces captured Judea and Samaria and called them the 'West Bank.' But the State of Israel survived.

Again in 1967 Arab nations around Israel banded together to destroy the Jewish state. Miraculously in six days the Lord returned Judea and Samaria to Israel, and gave them the Golan Heights, the Gaza strip and Sinai *(see the map on page 16)*. Clearly in their time of need **"the Lord was there,"** to bring about the fulfillment of His Word.

God gives warning to Islamic Arabic leaders, who want to possess Judea and Samaria.

*"Because you have said, 'These two nations and these two countries shall be mine, and we will possess them,' although **the Lord was there**... I will make myself known among them when I judge you."* *(Ezekiel 35:10)*

How did tiny Israel survive, against overwhelming opposition? The Lord promised to **be there** for Israel. He used the weakness of Israel to show His great power to save. Only the Lord can fulfill His Word in such miraculous ways.

In our day the Lord is keeping his promise to settle Jewish people on the mountains of Israel. Large Jewish settlements have been and are being built in Judea and Samaria. (Contrary to popular opinion there is still much vacant and desolate land in Judea and Samaria. Millions could settle here without displacing anyone.)

Those who fear God and who know His Word and His plan for the mountains of Israel understand that through Jewish settlement in the West Bank God is showing His faithfulness.

Those who try to stop the fulfillment of prophecy, stand against God.

Some people say that today's events in Israel are not a fulfillment of His Word. They believe that Israel must turn from sin before God's promises will be fulfilled. But the fact is that these promises **are** being fulfilled in ways that only God could bring about.

Israel was not sinless when God brought them out of Egypt. When they sinned, God punished them, but did not destroy them.

God brought the children of Israel out of Egypt to show the nations His power. When Israel sinned, if God had destroyed them in the wilderness the Egyptians would have said,

"He brought them out to harm them, to kill them in the mountains, and to consume them from the face of the earth?"   *(Exodus 32:12)*

Once again the Lord is bringing Israel into the Promised Land to show His great power. If He brought them out of the nations, and then destroyed them, the Egyptians, the Iraqis, the Syrians, the Jordanians, the Palestinians—many Moslems would say that the Lord brought Israel out to harm them—to consume them from the face of the earth.

As in the exodus from Egypt the return of Israel to the Land in our day is not a reward for good behavior. The return of Israel is not only a blessing for Israel, but a blessing for all nations—a blessing that no nation deserves.

By this great miracle, initiated by the Lord in the time of His choosing, He is showing His power and faithfulness to keep promises made thousands of years ago.

Russians Returning To Israel

Read Ezekiel chapter 36 carefully. There are no conditions which Israel must meet. *(Notice how seriously the Lord regards these promises. He has taken an oath.)*

> "*I have raised My hand in an oath...*
> *I will turn to you...*
> *I will multiply men...*
> *I will make you inhabited...*
> *I will cause men to walk on you...*
> *I had concern for My holy name...*
> *I will sanctify...*
> *I will take you...*
> *I will sprinkle...*
> *I will cleanse...*
> *I will give...*
> *I will put...*
> *I will deliver you...*
> *I will call for the grain and multiply it...*
> *I will multiply the fruit...*
> *I do this...*
> *I will increase their men like a flock...*
> *I, the LORD, have spoken it...*
> *I will do it...*   *(Ezekiel 36:7-36)*

Can the Lord speak more clearly? The Lord Himself is bringing Jewish people home and settling them in the mountains of Israel. Just as in His original promise to Abraham, there are no conditions. Israel **shall possess the mountains of Israel, because it is the will of the Lord.**

Why **did** the Lord,
- choose a people
- promise them a land
- let them fall into slavery in Egypt
- bring them out of Egypt
- resettle them in their Land
- exile them from their Land
- scatter them over the face of the earth
- promise to bring them back into their Land
- promise to make the desert blossom

Why **is** the Lord...
- bringing Jewish people home today
- making the desert bloom
- settling Jewish people in the Land including the West Bank

(Bible references for the above are included elsewhere.)

God **repeated** his purpose **59 times** in Ezekiel. He said,

"...*then you will know that I AM the...Lord.*"

This truth **must be accepted** before events in the Middle East can be understood.

This truth **must be accepted** before events in the Middle East can be understood.

People once asked, "How do we know there **is** a God? How do we know that the God of the Bible is the **ONLY GOD?** How do we know that the Bible is true? Some people worship other gods. How do we know that they are not worshiping the **'real'** God?"

The **God** of Abraham, Isaac, and Jacob **has proven His power and His reality through the survival of the Jewish people and the keeping of his promises**.

For nearly 2,000 years Israel suffered the curses of Deuteronomy 28 and Leviticus 26. Now God is keeping His promise to remember his covenant with them.

"...when they are in the land of their enemies, I will not cast them away, nor shall I abhor them, to utterly destroy them and break My covenant with them...."

"...I will remember the covenant of their ancestors, whom I brought out of the land of Egypt in the sight of the nations, that I might be their God...." *(Leviticus 26:44-45)*

The Lord promised to bring the Jewish people back, after they endured suffering *(Isaiah 40:2)*, but while they are yet sinful *(Ezekiel 36:24-25)*, and then to pour out His Spirit upon them and give them a new heart *(Ezekiel 36:26-27)*. *(More about this later.)*

Long ago the Lord caused promises to be recorded in the Bible, and in the sight of the entire world He is keeping His promises. No other being or group of beings could have accomplished what the Lord has done.

When we see the miraculous birth and surviva[1] of the tiny State of Israel and the lights of Jewish cities spreading over the mountain tops in the Promised Land, it is easy to believe in God today. What more proof is needed?

The God of Abraham, Isaac and Jacob **exists, and only He is Lord!**

As prophecies are fulfilled and the great power of God is revealed, these words from the Bible are important for the nations,

*"Blessed is he who blesses (Israel),
and cursed is he who curses (Israel)."*

(Numbers 24:9)

The Lord is sovereign. No one can prevent Him from doing His will. World powers that oppose God's plan can cause pain and suffering to their people, but they cannot prevent the Lord from keeping His promises. Regardless of what man does, God will keep His promises. Why not go for the blessing?

THE DESOLATE LAND

Before examining the Lord's promises and to appreciate what God has done, it is important to understand the situation in Israel prior to the return of large numbers of Jewish people.

Ezekiel prophesied that God would scatter the children of Israel throughout the nations and make the mountains of Israel desolate.

"...when you are scattered through the countries... I will...make the land...more desolate than the wilderness...."   *(Ezekiel 6:2,6,8,14)*

In 70 and 135 AD in fulfillment of His Word the Lord scattered the people of Israel around the world. A small remnant remained in the Land. For nearly 2,000 years the Promised Land lay desolate. Where once great forests stood, the hills were empty of trees and covered with rocks.

"The land was under Turkish control from 1517 to 1917, and Turkey destroyed this land thoroughly. The rulers enacted ridiculous laws; for example, one which required taxes to be paid for live trees. The people cut down the trees so they wouldn't have to pay taxes! This country therefore ended up in a truly wretched condition."[1]

The Land was described by Rev. Samuel Manning in 1874 in **Those Holy Fields**,

"...the Land is left void and desolate...without inhabitants."

[1]Unto Kunnas, *Kaarlo Syvanto—Pioneer: Forty years in Israel*, (Revised and updated from the original Finnish, Israel: 1988), 303-304.

25

Birthplaces of Moslems
Jerusalem—1931

For thousands of years Arabic people roamed over millions of square miles in the Middle East and Africa—unhindered by borders as we know them today. Bedouin frequently moved in and out of the area to find pasture for their flocks.

From the mid-1800's until 1948 jobs created by Jewish improvement of the land drew Arabs from other areas into the Holy Land. Therefore, many Moslems living in the Land before Israel became a state were **not** natives of Palestine. Below is a list of the birthplaces of Moslems living in the Jerusalem region as recorded in the census of 1931.

Albania
Algeria
Australia
Central America
Central Asiatic Territories
Cyprus
Egypt
Far Eastern Asia
France
Greece
Hejaz-Nejd
Indian Continent
Iraq
Morocco
Palestine
Persia (Iran)
South America
Spain
Syria
Transjordan
Tripoli
Tunis
Turkey
United Kingdom
USA
USSR
Yemen
Other Arabian Territories
Other African Territories

(See From Time Immemorial, by Joan Peters, p. 227)

Of course even during the worst desolation some people—Jewish, Arabic and others—remained in the Land.

"Jews did not entirely disappear from the Holy Land...Official records listed forty-three Jewish communities in the sixth century: twelve along the coast, in the Negev Desert and east of the Jordan River; and thirty-one in the Galilee and Jordan Valley."[2]

During Ottoman Turkish rule beginning in 1516 four holy cities were semi-autonomous Jewish areas—Jerusalem, Tiberias, Safed and Hebron.

In Tiberias *"A textile industry was set up, employing many Jews."[3]*

A report in 1864 indicated that the largest group of residents in Jerusalem were Jewish.

"The population of the City of Jerusalem is computed at 18,000 of whom about 5,000 are Moslems, 8,000 to 9,000 Jews, and the rest Christians of various denominations."[4]

Arabic people also lived in the Holy Land. Some were settled, but many were transient *(see page 26)*. During the past 2,000 years Arabic tribes roamed over more than 5,000,000 square miles in the Middle East and in northern Africa. For

---

[2]David Dolan, *Holy War for the Promised Land* (London: Hodder & Stoughton, 1991), 55-56.

[3]Ibid., 59.

[4]*Report on the Trade and Commerce of Jerusalem in the Year 1864*, March 1865 FO 195/808, in Hyamson, Consulate, 2, see Joan Peters, *From Time Immemorial* (New York: Harper & Row, Publishers, 1984), 336.

much of that time there were no borders as we know them today. They moved here and there for good pasture or for jobs.

*"We have seen strong evidence that the Holy Land was inhabited only sparsely in the nineteenth century. For centuries the non-Jewish, particularly the Muslim, peoples in the land had been largely composed of a revolving immigrant population...**the majority of those inhabitants were migrants and peasants originating from other lands....**"[5]*

While some Jewish, Arabic and others lived in the Holy Land in the late 1800's, the land was sparsely populated. *(See below.)*

Population Comparison

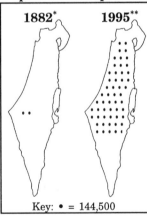

1882[*]   1995[**]

Key: • = 144,500

[*] The most reliable sources estimate the population in 1882 as about 289,000. *(See footnote 5 below.)* The accuracy of Martin Gilbert's estimates, which are sometimes cited, cannot be determined as no sources are given.

[**] The *CIA World Fact Book 1995* estimate for the population of Israel and the disputed areas is 7,566,447.

(The 1995 Israeli census shows 167,000 more for Israel proper than the CIA estimate.)

[5] Joan Peters, *From Time Immemorial* (New York: Harper & Row, Publishers, 1984), *"One historian deduced that of 141,000 settled Muslims living in all of Palestine (all areas) in 1882,"* at least 25%...were newcomers or descendants of those who arrived after 1831 (Egyptian conquest) pp. 196-197. *"The British consul (1859) complained that there were too few inhabitants of any sort in Palestine. 'Palestine,' he reported, was almost 'empty of inhabitants,' and urgently needed a 'body of population irrespective of religious considerations'"* pp. 198-199 *(Also see p. 244).*

"...(R)oughly 200,000 Muslims were living in all of Western Palestine in 1882" (65,000 nomadic and 135,000 settled) plus 55,000 Christians and 34,000 Jews. (Joan Peters, *From Time Immemorial*, p 244 from statistics of Vital Cuinet for 1895. Also see *Murray's Handbook for Travellers in Syria and Palestine*, 1858, which was reprinted in the *Encyclopaedia Britannica*, 8th edition, 1860, vol. XX, p. 905,)

In 1866 in **The Land and the Book** W. M. Thompson said,

"How melancholy is this utter desolation! Not a house, not a trace of inhabitants, not even shepherds...to relieve the dull monotony...Isaiah says that Sharon (coastal area in Israel) shall be wilderness, and...(it) has become a sad and impressive reality."

Mark Twain toured the country in the 1860's. He wrote in **Innocents Abroad**,

"...the hallowed spot where the shepherds watched their flocks by night, and where the angels sang, 'Peace on earth, good will to men,' is **untenanted by any living creature***...and the 'desert places' around about them...sleep in the hush of a solitude that is inhabited only by birds of prey and skulking foxes."*

The Word of the Lord proved true.

"...your land shall be desolate...."
(Leviticus 26:33)

The once fertile Jezreel Valley was a swampland infested with deadly mosquitoes.

"During the Turkish occupation...the flat land of Jisreel, in the middle of Israel...about fifty kilometers long and ten kilometers wide...was so greatly infested with malaria that thousands of people died, especially during the time when no effective medicine to cure this disease was known. The Jews did a tremendously effective job of draining the Jisreel Valley, which the Bible calls Armageddon, and where the decisive battle in the history of the world will be fought."[6]

Sand smothered Israel's coastal plain. The mountains were barren mounds of rocks. **Because of the desolation, returning Jewish people could settle in most of the Holy Land without displacing anyone.**

"Here, once again, we see God's foresight and wisdom. If this land had been well cultivated and well settled, there wouldn't have been room for the Jews to come here when the time came for God to return them to their own land."[7]

[6]Unto Kunnas, Kaarlo Syvanto--*Pioneer: Forty years in Israel, (Revised and updated from the original Finnish, Israel: 1988),* 304-305.

[7]*Ibid. 30*

A century ago Israel was barren

PROMISES

The Lord made promises to the mountains of Israel.

- **Israel will return**
- **You will shoot forth branches and yield fruit**
- **You will be tilled and sown**
- **I will multiply the house of Israel on you**
- **The cities will be inhabited**
- **The ruins will be rebuilt**
- **Israel will possess you**   *(Ezekiel 36:8-12)*

Israel Will Return

In the mid-to-late 19th century increasing numbers of Jews began to return to the Land. The barren Land took the lives of many of the early settlers through sickness and overwork as they drained swamps and planted trees.

In 1920 the League of Nations designated British-occupied Palestine as a homeland for the Jewish people.

Jewish settlements created jobs. **Arabic workers from neighboring lands were drawn to the area for jobs.** As Jewish settlements grew, Arabic settlements grew up around them.

The rise of Hitler caused more Jewish people to return to the Land. But Moslem complaints and terrorism persuaded England to reduce the number of Jews allowed to return at a time when more than six-million needed to escape Nazi extermination camps.

In 1948 Israel became a State. For the first time in 2,000 years Jews could return to the Land unhindered. Since then millions of Jewish people have returned.

Return from Ethiopia _____

In 1991 almost 15,000 Ethiopian Jews were air lifted into Israel in two days *(Operation Solomon)*. Ethiopians managed to come to Israel by crossing the wastelands of Africa on foot to Sudan. Edna Yeholashet of Ethiopia gave this account to the Jerusalem Post Magazine as reported on May 22, 1992.

"Edna Yeholashet's eldest sister simply disappeared one day in 1984. She had left Ateye village...to attend school...and didn't return. 'She never said goodby'

"...the youth of her...neighborhood started disappearing...it was always without saying goodby

"'At the age of 14, when all the children my age had left the village, I decided to go, too', Edna said, 'I told my mother "I can't be the only Jew in my class. The non-Jews attack me."'

"'She was (unhappy) at the thought of leaving ....but she had to fulfill the dream of seeing Jerusalem.

"The group left at night. All walking had to be done at night...During the day, they hid in holes and caves. The heat was intolerable and their water soon ran out...they came to a village to restock, but were recognized as Jews, and had to flee for their lives. 'The guides told us to escape over a high mountain because the villagers wanted to kill us. To my dying day, I'll never forget how we ran.'

"Another time, robbers armed with axes tried to attack them and they had to hide from ravenous lions. But the worst nightmare was her feeling that 'I would never see my mother again.'

Yemenites Also Risked Their Lives to Come to Israel

"On the last day, Edna fainted. They had been hiding in a blazing hot cave. She and a friend went to seek shade under a tree. 'The guides told us that in one hour we would reach the refugee camp in Sudan, so we washed with our last water. Then we heard that it would take another day. When we came to the tree there were five bodies covered with leaves. The stench was unbelievable. I wanted to lie down and die, too. I fainted.'

"The next day...they stumbled, famished and dehydrated, into the Red Cross camp in Sudan.

"After seven months...(and) for the first time in her life, Edna boarded a plane...and landed in Israel...She was reunited with her mother and brother just before Operation Solomon, and today the family is scattered throughout Israel."

Morocco

"...(From) North Africa, more than 300,000 Jews have crowded into Israel since 1948. Almost 250,000 of them arrived from what is now Morocco where Jews have lived since 586 BC."[1]

Tunisia

"...Of 105,000 Jews in 1948 (in Tunisia) 50,000 emigrated to Israel"[2]

See notes 1 through 8 on page 43

Iraq

"...There were more than 130,000 Jews in Iraq in 1947"...(at this time) "all Iraqi Jews who went to Palestine and did not return would be tried in absentia as criminals. Those who were tried in absentia were sentenced to hang or to serve extended prison sentences.

"...In 1949 all bank accounts held by Jews were frozen...Palestinian Arabs, many militantly anti-Jewish were given the Jewish public buildings and the vacant former living quarters of Jewish escapees."

"...In 1950 Iraq enacted a law that allowed Jews to 'leave for good.' The Jews left their...accumulated holdings behind, and within the first three years of the law most of them were flown to Israel, with the Iraqi government taking 'a handsome share of the profits' produced by the flights.

"...Between 1969 and 1973 at least 17 Jews were hanged in a public square. Twenty-six others were slaughtered in their homes or in Iraqi prisons. As of 1982 most of Iraq's Jewry had found refuge in Israel."[3]

Egypt

In Egypt "...when the six-day war began, Jews were arrested and held in concentration camps, where they were beaten and whipped, deprived

See notes 1 through 8 on page 43

of water for days on end and forced to chant anti-Israel slogans."

"...By 1970, these Jews too had escaped the country. 'Egypt,' according to the officer in charge of the internment camp, '...had no place for Jews.'"[4]

Syria

"...In Syria in early 1947, only 13,000 Jews remained; thousands more Jewish refugees had fled many of them covertly, and the Syrian government, according to the New York Herald Tribune, April 14, 1947, launched 'an investigation into the disappearance of some 17,000 Syrian Jews since the last government census [1943].'"[5]

Returning to Israel from Yemen

Yemen

"...Nearly 50,000 Yemenites who had never seen a plane were airlifted to Israel in 1949 and 1950. Since the Book of Isaiah promised 'They shall mount up with wings as eagles,' the Jewish community boarded the 'eagles' contentedly; to the pilot's consternation some of them lit a bonfire aboard, to cook their food!"[6]

These accounts of the exodus of Jewish people from Moslem countries are only a tiny glimpse of the entire picture of the return of Israel. The complete story would fill many volumes.

The most spectacular return to the Land began when the Soviet Union suddenly collapsed. For many years Jewish people called 'Refuseniks' struggled for the right to leave Russia to live in Israel. Many were imprisoned. The breakup of the Soviet Union freed them and hundreds of thousands more to realize their dream of living in Israel. *(Russia is north of Israel.)*

Return from the North

"...'the days are coming,' says the Lord 'that they shall no longer say, "As the Lord lives who brought up the children of Israel from the land of Egypt," *but, "As the Lord lives who brought up and led the descendants of the house of Israel from the* **north country** *and from all the countries where I had driven them." And they shall dwell in their own Land.'"* *(Jeremiah 23:7-8)*

See notes 1 through 8 on page 43

The return from the north was prophesied 2,500 years ago. Hundreds of thousands from the former USSR have arrived in Israel. An additional one to two million are expected.

The Lord said,

"Behold, I will bring (the children of Israel) **from the north country***...a great throng shall return...with weeping."* *(Jeremiah 31:8-9)*

Flights arranged by the Jewish Agency arrive from the former Soviet Union daily. Christian organizations have also helped. Dozens of plane loads of Jewish immigrants from the north were

Russians Returning to Israel From the 'North'

financed by Christians. They also financed
several ship loads of Jewish immigrants. On the
ships immigrants were allowed to bring personal
items—even cars.

Is this the beginning of the great exodus from
the north, which will be greater than the
exodus from Egypt? Many say, 'Yes.'

You Will
Shoot Forth Branches and Yield Fruit

The Turkish tree tax had caused great barrenness by the 19th century. Some sources say that
less than 1,000 trees were left in the Land.

But the Lord promised that the Land would once
again shoot forth branches.

*"But you, O mountains of Israel, you shall shoot
forth your branches and yield your fruit to My
people Israel, for they are about to come."*
(Ezekiel 36:8)

From 1906 to 1990 Jewish settlers and visitors
to Israel planted 256,000,000 trees in Israel. Today
forests are spreading across the Land. Orange
and grapefruit trees grow in the plains along the
coast. Banana plants and date palms bear fruit
in the Jordan valley.

You Will Be Tilled and Sown

*"I will turn to you, and you shall be tilled and
sown."* *(Ezekiel 36:9)*

Where swamps were drained, grains, cotton, flowers and vegetables now grow in fertile fields. Each year corn and wheat fields are pushing farther south into the desert. Isaiah spoke of this time.

"...the desert shall rejoice and blossom as the rose...waters shall burst forth in the wilderness and streams in the desert. The parched ground shall become a pool, and the thirsty land springs of water...." (Isaiah 35:1,6-7)

In 1992 record breaking rain and snow in Israel caused waters to burst forth in the wilderness and streams to run through the desert. In the spring the hills in the desert were carpeted with grass and flowers.

"After this winter's deluge, the entire desert has become a flower garden. There is not only green but shades of green splashed with red and yellow and violet."[7]

Ben Gurion, the first Prime Minister of Israel, dreamed of seeing this day. He lived in Sde Boker, a kibbutz *(settlement)*, which experiments with agriculture in one of the most barren deserts on earth—the Desert of Zin in southern Israel.

Professor Issar, of Sde Boker, and his associates are known around the world for advances in desert agriculture. They rediscovered ancient farming methods. For example three thousand years ago dams were built in low places to hold rain water. Grain grew in these low areas.

See notes 1 through 8 on page 43

Israelis use several versions of this idea, such as the following, rain water is trapped in shallow ponds. It soaks into the ground. Eucalyptus trees are planted in the ponds, surviving severe desert conditions. The shade of the trees allows smaller plants to grow. In time evaporation from the trees will affect the climate and increase the amount of rainfall in the area. Gradually the desert is being reclaimed.

New methods of irrigation save water. In one method water is carried to each plant in plastic hoses. In the past irrigation water ran in open canals or was sprayed into the air. Much of the water evaporated before it reached the roots of plants. By running water in hoses directly to each plant and allowing it to drip slowly on the ground under the plant, much precious water is saved.[8]

These new methods have blessed the world. Many nations are learning from Israel to grow crops on arid land. Small amounts of water are producing food for more people.

"...in your (Isaac's) seed all the nations of the earth shall be blessed."   *(Genesis 26:4)*

This promise of the Lord has been fulfilled in many ways. The entire world has been blessed spiritually through Isaac's seed. It was through Isaac's seed *(the Jewish people)* that the nations of the earth received the Bible. And from the Jewish people Jesus was born. Now the nations are blessed in physical ways as well.

See notes 1 through 8 on page 43

Israel Will Possess the Mountains of Israel

The Lord said to the mountains of Israel,

"I will cause men to walk on you, My people Israel; they shall take possession of you...."
(Ezekiel 36:12)

In 1967 in a miraculous six-day war, this promise of God came true—Israel took possession of the mountains of Israel, including the Old City of Jerusalem.

Jerusalem which occupied one tiny mountaintop in King David's day, now spreads for miles over many mountains.

"...Jerusalem shall be inhabited as towns without walls, because of the multitude of men and livestock in it."
(Zechariah 2:4)

Today Jerusalem is a city without walls. At night the lights of the city look like the stars that Abraham tried to count *(see Genesis 15:5).*

I Will Multiply Israel on You...
Cities Will Be Inhabited...
Ruins Rebuilt

"I will multiply men upon you, all the house of Israel...the cities shall be inhabited and the ruins rebuilt...."
(Ezekiel 36:10)

Jewish people lived in the so-called West Bank *(Judea and Samaria)* when Israel was attacked by six Arabic Islamic nations in 1948. Jewish communities in the captured area were destroyed by Arab Forces. When Israel recaptured the West Bank in 1967, the communities were rebuilt.

Jewish communities, destroyed in 1948 are back on the map, for example,
* **The Jewish Quarter of the Old City**
* **Gush Etzion is today Kfar Ezyon.**
* **Kallia is Qalya.**
* **Bet Haarava is Bet haArava.**
* **Atarot is the site of the Jerusalem Airport.**
* **Neve Yakov is rebuilt.**

Ancient Jewish sites are flourishing again....
* **The modern town of Shilo** *(I Samuel 1:3)* **is thriving.**
* **Bethel is Bet El.** *(Genesis 35:15)*
* **Mount Gaash** *(Joshua 24:30)* **supports the city of Ariel** *(population 15,000).*
* **Kiriat Arba** *(Joshua 20:7)* **is now a Jewish town near Hebron.**
* **and others too numerous to mention.**

NOTES (Pages 31-43)
[1]Joan Peters, *From Time Immemorial* (New York: Harper & Row, Publishers, 1984), 50.
[2]Ibid., 60
[3]Ibid., 45-46
[4]Ibid., 50
[5]Ibid.
[6]Ibid., 41
[7]*The Jerusalem Post Magazine,* March 27, 1992
[8]Lecture by Dr. Issar at Sde Boker in June, 1989

LOCATION OF ANCIENT EDOM

Mediterranean Sea

(French Occupied)
Syria

British-Occupied area (1917-1948)
PALESTINE

Site of Ancient
EDOM
in the Mount Seir region

• **Bozrah**

• **Teman**

Gulf of Elat

Red Sea

*The location of the ancient land of **Edom** is shown in the borders of the former British-held area which was known as '**Palestine**'.*

Over the years the boundries of Edom expanded and contracted—sometimes reaching as far south as the Gulf of Elat

*Although Palestine was never a sovereign state, in recent years some Arabic people from this area call themselves '**Palestinians**'.*

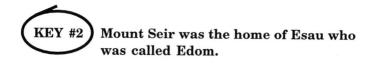
MOUNT SEIR

*Son of man, set your face against Mount Seir
and prophesy against it, and say to it...
Thus says the Lord God, Behold, O Mount Seir, I am
against you and I will stretch out my hand against you....*
(Ezekiel 35:2-3)

Mount Seir was the homeland of Esau *(also called Edom)* father of the Edomites. We know this because the Bible says,

"So Esau dwelt in Mount Seir. Esau is Edom."
(Genesis 36:8)

Esau is one of the ancestors of the Arabic people. *(see page 51)*

Bible Names	Today Called
Mount Seir, Edom, Esau, Amalek, Ishmael Ammon, Lot, Moab	Arabic people or nations, Jordanian, and/or Palestinian
Jacob, Judah, or Israel	Israel, or Jewish People
Palestine	Jordan (77%) and Israel (23%)

45

Notice that the Lord speaks to an area called Edom or Mount Seir. This is the area where the ancient Edomites lived. Arabic people—descendants of ancient Middle East tribes such as Edom—still live there today.

ANCIENT EDOM IN JORDAN

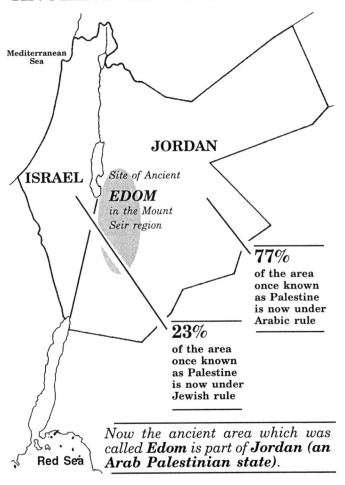

Mediterranean Sea

JORDAN

ISRAEL

Site of Ancient

EDOM

in the Mount Seir region

77% of the area once known as Palestine is now under Arabic rule

23% of the area once known as Palestine is now under Jewish rule

Red Sea

*Now the ancient area which was called **Edom** is part of **Jordan** (an Arab Palestinian state).*

KEY #3 Today people living in the area once known as Edom are called Arabs, Jordanians and/or Palestinians.

Where was Edom? After World War I, the land known long ago as Edom was part of the area called Palestine. *(See page 44.)*

Was Palestine a state?

No, never.

Then what was Palestine?

After World War I, the British occupied land in the Middle East. Palestine was the popular name of one area in their control.

According to most reliable sources, Palestine is an English name derived from the Roman name Palaestina. When the Romans captured Judea in the first century, they called it Syria Palaestina—some believe to erase any Jewish connection to the land and to insult the Jews by using a name derived from the Philistines, Israel's ancient enemies during the time of King Saul and King David.[1]

Who are the Palestinians?

Until 1948 residents in the area were called 'Palestinians,' and were **NOT** a separate race. All residents of the area *(Jews, Gentiles and Arabs)* were Palestinians. However, at that time Arabic people preferred not to be called Palestinian.

Today most people who identify themselves as Palestinians are Arabic. However, even today not all Arab residents of Israel and the territories wish to be called Palestinians.

[1] See David Dolan, *Holy War for the Promised Land* (London: Hodder & Stoughton, 1991), 55.

The former British-occupied area called Palestine
is now two states—Jordan 77% *(ruled by Arabs);*
and Israel 23% *(under Jewish rule—see map on
page 46).* The area, that was known as Edom in
ancient times, is now part of Jordan.

The history of Jordan and the so-called Arab
Palestinians fits the situation described in Ezekiel chapters 35 and 36. (More about this later.)

*Note: Regarding the location of Edom, one group mistakenly teaches that Edom
is Turkey. As if to guard against this and similar errors, the Lord uses several
ways of pinpointing Edom. For example in chapter 35 of Ezekiel He speaks of
Mount Seir, which is south of the Dead Sea. In Jeremiah 49:7-22 He mentions
Teman (also see Obadiah v. 9) and Bozrah. These cities were also located south
of the Dead Sea in what is now Jordan (see page 44). Israel walked around
Edom to get to the Jordan River across from Jericho. In light of this, one look
at a map of the Middle East shows that Turkey cannot be Edom.*

The Arabic People

The Bible tells us that Esau lived in the region of
Mount Seir and Edom. He was one of the
ancestors of the Arabic people.

How do we define 'Arabic'? In this work Arabic is
used as it is used in everyday language. An Arab
is anyone who identifies himself as Arabic.

In Bible times an Arab was a descendant of
Ishmael who lived in Arabia. But Ishmael inter-
married with other tribes. For example Esau
(Edom) was Ishmael's son-in-law. Esau married
Ishmael's daughters, Basemath *(Genesis 36:2-3)*
and Mahalath. *(Genesis 28:8-9). See the chart on page 51.*

In the time of Ishmael and Esau the ancestors of

today's Arabic people were many tribes as were the ancestors of today's Jewish people. Through four thousand years of intermarriage the tribes disappeared. Today many *(if not most)* Jewish people do not know which of the sons of Jacob is their ancestor. An individual could be related to all twelve tribes.

The same is true of Arabic people. Arabic ancestors intermarried with one another for 4,000 years. The Ishmaelite, Edomite, Moabite, Midianite, Ammonite, and Temanite tribes have disappeared. Today people identifying themselves as Arabic occupy five million square miles across the ancient homelands of Ishmael, Edom, Moab, Midian, Ammon and across North Africa.

Arabic and Jewish people are cousins *(see pages 50-51)*. Arabic people are also related to the Egyptians, because Ishmael's mother Hagar was an Egyptian and he married a woman from Egypt *(see Genesis 21:21)*.

Josephus

Josephus mentions a group of Edomites, called Idumaeans, who were driven out of their land into the desert and later were absorbed into Israel. Some believe that all of Edom converted to Judaism at that time.

However, the ancient peoples had intermarried for 2,000 years before the event that Josephus records. Is it reasonable to assume that every person descended from Esau was killed or converted to Judaism at that time? Probably not.

Jewish Ancestors

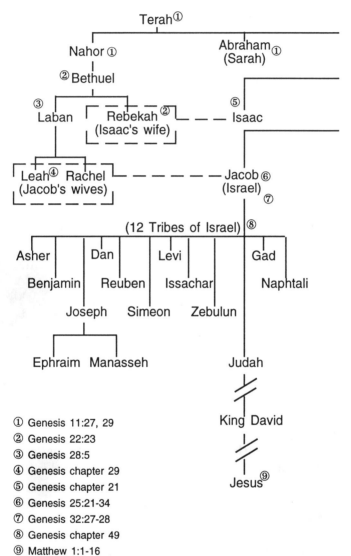

① Genesis 11:27, 29
② Genesis 22:23
③ Genesis 28:5
④ Genesis chapter 29
⑤ Genesis chapter 21
⑥ Genesis 25:21-34
⑦ Genesis 32:27-28
⑧ Genesis chapter 49
⑨ Matthew 1:1-16

Note: In Bible times the children of Israel were known by their tribe. After many thousands of years of intermarriage, most families do not know their tribe. Today all of the descendants of Israel are called Jewish (in English) after Judah (Jacob's son), or Israel (the name the Lord gave to Jacob).

50

Arabic Ancestors

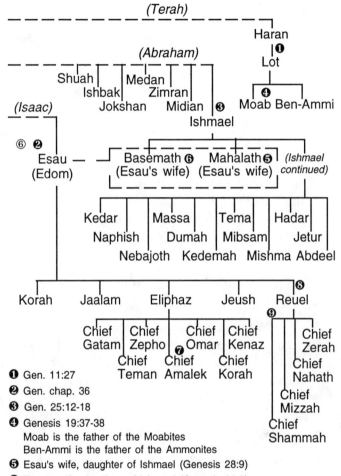

(Terah)

Haran
| ❶
Lot

(Abraham)

Shuah | Medan
Ishbak | Zimran
(Isaac)   Jokshan   Midian | ❸   Moab Ben-Ammi
Ishmael

⑥ ❷

Esau —
(Edom)

Basemath ❻   Mahalath ❺   *(Ishmael*
(Esau's wife) (Esau's wife)   *continued)*

Kedar | Massa | Tema | Hadar
Naphish | Dumah | Mibsam | Jetur
Nebajoth   Kedemah   Mishma   Abdeel

| ❽

Korah   Jaalam   Eliphaz   Jeush   Reuel

❾

Chief | Chief | Chief | Chief
Gatam | Zepho | ❼ Omar | Kenaz
Chief   Chief   Chief
Teman   Amalek   Korah

Chief
Zerah
Chief
Nahath
Chief
Mizzah
Chief
Shammah

❶ Gen. 11:27

❷ Gen. chap. 36

❸ Gen. 25:12-18

❹ Genesis 19:37-38
Moab is the father of the Moabites
Ben-Ammi is the father of the Ammonites

❺ Esau's wife, daughter of Ishmael (Genesis 28:9)

❻ Esau's wife, daughter of Ishmael (Genesis 36:3)

❼ Amalek is believed to be the father of the Amalekites
(Deuteronomy 25:17)

❽ Grandson of Ishmael and son of Esau (Genesis 36:3,17)

❾ Great Grandsons of Ishmael and grandsons of Esau (Genesis
36:17)

Note: These cousins of the Israelis lived in adjoining areas in the
Middle East. Intermarriage melted them into one group which we call
Arabs. Arabic people now rule 17 countries in the Middle East and
North Africa.

Individual Arabic People

Some point out that individual people of Arabic descent live as Jews and Gentiles, and some Jewish and Gentile people live as Arabs. Through the ages some have moved from one group to the other as Ruth the Moabitess did. This does not affect the identity of the group.

Islam

Most Arabic people are Moslems practising a religion called Islam. Moslems dominate the Arab countries. Most Arab leaders who try to destroy Israel are Moslems. Many terrorists have come out of this group.

Christians of Arabic Descent

Christians of Arabic descent have accepted the Jewish Messiah as Savior. Since they believe in the Bible, Israel's existence should not be a problem. Many Christians of Arabic descent live in harmony with Israel. Some are Israeli citizens, who serve in the regular police force or in the Israeli Defence Forces (IDF), defending their country like other Israelis.

Palestinians

As stated earlier, between 1917 and 1948 Palestinian meant anyone (Jewish, Arabic and others) living in the British-occupied area called Palestine. Now most people who call themselves Palestinians are Arab Moslems.

The Rest of the Nations All Around

In chapter 36 of Ezekiel other nations are mentioned in addition to Edom. They are called *'the rest of the nations'* or *'the rest of the nations all around.'* These nations are included in the condemnation of Edom. The *rest of the nations* are mentioned three times,

*"...I have spoken... against **the rest of the nations** and against all Edom"*   *(Ezekiel 36:5)*

*"...you became the possession of the **rest of the nations"***   *(Ezekiel 36:3)*

*"...which became plunder and mockery to the **rest of the nations all around"***   *(Ezekiel 36:4)*

These verses speak of a group of nations that will band together against Israel.

Notice in verse 4, *the rest of the nations* are *all around* the mountains of Israel. Psalm 83 mentions nations and peoples who band together against Israel, and when they are put on a map, we find that they are *all around* the mountains of Israel. *(See the map on page 54)*

Compare Ezekiel 36:3-5 with the following,

*"...**They** have taken crafty counsel **together** against Your sheltered ones. **They** have said, 'Come, and let **us** cut them off from being a nation, that the name of Israel may be remembered no more.' for **they** have consulted **together** with one consent; **they form a confederacy** against You"*   *(Psalm 83:3-5)*

53

The Rest of the Nations All Around

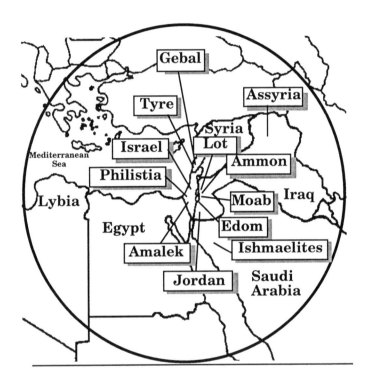

In the next verse is a list of peoples and nations headed by *Edom*.

Edom	*Ishmaelites*	*Amalek*
Moab	*Ammon*	*Lot*
Tyre	*Assyria*	*Philistia*
Gebal	*Hagrites*	

Six or seven of these peoples *(Edom, Ishmaelites, Amalek, Moab, Ammon, Lot and perhaps Hagrites)* are listed among the Arabic ancestors. *(see p. 51)*.

The other peoples mentioned lived in what are

now Arab Islamic nations or areas. Assyria was in Iraq. Tyre and possibly Gebal were in Lebanon. The Philistines were from Philistia. *(While there are no longer Philistines, Palestinians take their name from them.)*

Like the nations of Ezekiel 36:3-5 the ancient people listed above, who would join together to destroy Israel, were *all around* the mountains of Israel.

Compare the following passage, *"Come, and let us cut them off from being a nation, that the name of Israel may be remembered no more."* *(Psalm 83:4)* with some of the statements made by nations that are *all around* Israel today.

Egypt—*"I announce from here, on behalf of the United Arab Republic people, that this time we will exterminate Israel."*

Notice above the threat to *"exterminate* Israel."

The statement from Egypt also mentions the *United Arab Republic people (a confederacy of Egypt and Syria [1958-1961]).* Compare this with,

"...they form a confederacy against You"
(Psalm 83:5)

Following are more statements by peoples *around* Israel.

Iraq—*"Our goal is clear—to wipe Israel off the map"*

Libya—*"The battle with Israel must be such that after it, Israel will cease to exist."*

55

PLO *(Palestinians)—"The struggle...is not about Israel's borders, but about Israel's existence."*

Egypt—*"Arabs do not cease to act for the extermination of Israel."*

(Sources are listed when these statements and others are quoted later in this work.)

Mount Seir, Edom and *the nations around Israel* in chapters 35 and 36 of Ezekiel and Psalm 83 refer to the leaders of Arab Islamic groups and nations who are trying to destroy Israel.

Something to keep in mind

God is always merciful. The psalmist calls on God to punish Edom and the *nations all around.* But the punishment has a purpose,

*"...That they may **seek Your name**, O Lord...That they may know that **You**, whose name alone is the Lord, **are the Most High** over all the earth."*
(Psalm 83:16,18)

In the following pages as we read about the sins of Edom and *the rest of the nations all around,* please understand that the Lord wants to bring Arabic people, who are deceived by Islam, to acknowledge Him as Lord. He hopes that they will seek Him.

This must be our attitude too. Please remember that most Arabic people are Moslems and do not have the Bible. Most do not understand that they are offending the Lord when they attack Israel.

Young Arabic people who are trying to live good lives are told by Islamic religious leaders that they will be in paradise if they are killed while fighting against Israel.

While we must not condemn Arabic people for their blindness, neither should we encourage them to oppose the plan of God.

Some well-meaning, but uninformed Jewish and Christian people encourage the Palestinians to claim sovereignty over the Lord's Land—to strive for a second Palestinian state. They think they are being unselfishly just. But in reality they are misleading Palestinians by encouraging them to oppose God. Believers are responsible to know the Word of God and to warn their Arabic brothers to walk in harmony with the Lord's plan.

Note: While the Bible teaches that Israel will possess the Holy Land, aliens are allowed to live in Israel under Israeli rule (see Ezekiel 11:23). Today thousands of Palestinians live in peace under Israeli law. They have homes and jobs in Israel. Some even sit as representatives in the Israeli Knesset (Congress or Parliament).

A young Arabic woman who teaches Arabic in an Israeli school is grateful that free Israeli education has given her the opportunity to teach. When her mother was young, the family lived in Judea under Jordanian rule. No universities were available in the Jordanian-occupied area. This lovely young Palestinian woman said, "Israel is the best country in the world."

57

When the disputed areas were closed, a young Palestinian father, who builds stone walls, was forced to work for a company owned by an oil-rich Arab country. Instead of the NIS 70 ($23) per day he received while working in Israel, his pay was NIS 20 ($7) per day. He told us that he did not want to live in a Palestinian State. Although he is Arabic, he preferred to live in Israel.

While other Arabic individuals (especially the older generation that can remember living under Jordanian rule) agree, it is dangerous to say so. Masked Arabic Islamic terrorists in PLO and Hamas organizations at times torture and kill as many as 3 to 10 Palestinians a week for 'collaborating' with Israel. In recent months more and more Arabs are finding the courage to speak out against Palestinian Authority rights abuses.

Islamic leaders set themselves against God and take the lives of those Arabic people among them who wish to live in peace with Israel.

Why is God Against Edom?

In chapter 35 of Ezekiel the Lord tells **Edom** that He is against them because,
- They hated Israel since ancient times (v. 5)
- They shed the blood of Israel (v. 5)
- They want Israel's Land (v. 10)
- They spoke blasphemies (v. 12)
- They boasted against the Lord (v. 13)

In the sections which follow we look at events in history which support the charges made by the Lord in chapter 35.

AN ANCIENT HATRED

*"Thus says the Lord God...behold O **Mount Seir,** I am against you; I will stretch out My hand against you...because you have had an **ancient hatred....**"* *(Ezekiel 35:3,5)*

Remember that **Mount Seir** was the home of Esau and was called **Edom.** In the quotation above God confronts Edom for having an ancient hatred. How and when did this ancient hatred begin?

Esau "Despised His Birthright"

The Bible tells us that almost four thousand years ago (1,700 BC) Esau despised his birthright and sold it to his brother Jacob for a bowl of stew. The Bible says,

*"Jacob cooked a stew...Esau said...'Please feed me with (the) stew'...Jacob said, 'Sell me your birthright'...Esau said, 'Look, I am about to die; so what is this birthright to me?'...So he swore to him, and sold his birthright to Jacob...he ate and drank, arose, and went his way. Thus Esau **despised his birthright....**"* *(Genesis 25:29-34)*

Later Isaac gave Jacob his blessing. When Esau discovered that Jacob had both the birthright and the blessing, jealousy filled his heart and he hated Jacob. **Esau planned to kill Jacob** *(Genesis 27:41).* Isaac and Rebekah, sent Jacob away *(Genesis 27:42-28:9).*

God changed Jacob's name to Israel *(Genesis 32:28)*. His descendants were called the Children of Israel.

Edom

Moses led the Children of Israel out of slavery in Egypt to the Promised Land. The children of Israel trudged for 40 years through the wilderness. As they neared the lands of their cousins, the descendants of Esau *(Edom)* and Lot *(Moab)*, the Lord told Israel not to attack them *(see Deuteronomy 2:4-8,19)*.

Moses asked permission from the King of Edom to pass through his land. The King of **Edom** met Moses with an army. Messengers from Moses said to the King of Edom,

"Thus says your brother Israel, 'You know all the hardship that has befallen us...Please let us pass through your country ...'"   *(Numbers 20:14)*

"Edom said, 'You shall not pass through my land....'   *(Numbers 20:18)*

"The children of Israel said, 'We will go by the Highway, and if I or my livestock drink any of your water, then I will pay for it; let me only pass through on foot, nothing more.' Then he said, 'You shall not pass through.' So Edom came out against them with many men and with a strong hand. Thus Edom refused to give Israel passage through his territory; so Israel turned away from him."
       (Numbers 20:18-21)

The Israelites circled around Edom.

Hundreds of years later the tribes of Edom, Moab and Ammon gathered in the oasis of En Gedi (south of Jerusalem) to attack King Jehoshaphat and Judah. When Jehoshaphat appealed to God, He promised Judah victory.

Jehoshaphat appointed certain people to go before the army of Judah singing praises to God. The army of Judah found the enemy soldiers dead in a valley between En Gedi and Jerusalem.

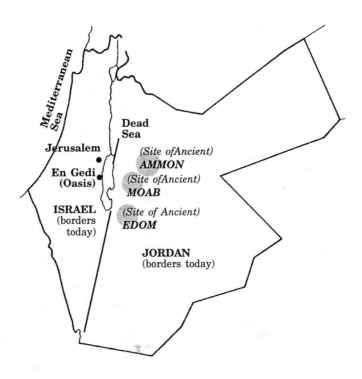

ATTACK ON JUDAH

Edom, Ammon and Moab

Hundreds of years after the exodus from Egypt **Edom**, Ammon, and Moab *(three ancient ancestors of the Arabic people)* still despised Israel. *(At this time Israel was split in two. The kingdom in the north was called Israel and the southern kingdom was called Judah.)* In the time of King Jehoshaphat, who ruled the southern kingdom, Edom, Ammon and Moab *(Compare with the list of nations on page 54)* joined together to destroy Judah *(the Jewish people)*. Jehoshaphat appealed to God and said,

*"... (H)ere are the people of Ammon, Moab, and **Mount Seir (Edom)**—whom you would not let Israel invade when they came out of the land of Egypt, but they turned from them and did not destroy them—here they are, rewarding us by coming to throw us out of Your possession which You have given us to inherit."*

(2 Chronicles 20:10-11)

Jehoshaphat and the Jewish people humbled themselves before the Lord and the Lord saved them. They trusted in the Lord and went to meet the Arabic ancestral tribes singing praises to the Lord. When they arrived, the enemy soldiers lay dead in the valley *(see 2 Chronicles 20:24)*. The Edomite, Moabite and Ammonite armies had destroyed one another.

The ancient hatred spoken of by God can be traced throughout Bible times. And it has continued in this century and to our day.

School Days

Hatred Was (is?) Taught in Schools

Schools in some Arabic countries taught children to hate Jewish people. The following quotes are from official Ministry of Education materials,[1]

Jordan

"Jordan, 1966, for third-year junior high school: MODERN WORLD HISTORY, For example,

'The Jews in Europe were persecuted and despised because of their corruption, meanness and treachery.'"

"Jordan, 1964, department for school curricula and textbooks - 1st year High School GLANCES AT ARAB SOCIETY, p. 117. An exercise:

'Israel was born to die. Prove it.'"

Syria

"Syria, Damascus, 1963-64, for second-year junior high school: THE RELIGIOUS ORDINANCES READER, p. 138. For example:

[1] Joan Peters, *From Time Immemorial*, 79

'The Jews...lived exiled and despised since by their nature they are vile, greedy and enemies of mankind.'"

"Syria, 1963, fifth-year elementary school: BASIC SYNTAX AND SPELLING. An exercise.

'We Shall Expel All the Jews.' For example, 'Analyze the following sentences:...2. We shall expel all the Jews from the Arab countries.'"

Death Camp during the Holocaust

Egypt

"Egypt, 1965, Egyptian State Seal, 1st year Junior High school: GRAMMAR, p. 244. An exercise:

'The Arabs do not cease to act for the extermination of Israel.'"

"U.A.R. (Egypt), for ninth-grade secondary schools: ZIONIST IMPERIALISM, by Abbad Muhmud Al-Akkad, p. 249.

'...Israel shall not live if the Arabs stand fast in their hatred...Even if all the human race, and the devil in Hell, conspire to aid her, she shall not exist.'"

Hatred was reinforced in adults. In 1973 the Egyptian writer Anis Mansour wrote,

"People all over the world have come to realize that Hitler was right...the whole world... has...expelled them and despised them... and burnt them in Hitler's crematoria... Would that he had finished it!" [2]

The **ancient hatred** was systematically and deliberately taught to children in public schools. Those who learned to hate Israel are in terrible danger. To them God says,

*"I am against you; I will stretch out My hand against you...because you have had an **ancient hatred**".* *(Ezekiel 35:3-5)*

---

[2] *Al-Akhbar,* August 19, 1973.

They Shed the Blood of Israel

The Lord said,

"...(You) shed the blood of the children of Israel...at the time of their calamity...." *(Ezekiel 35:4-5)*

Jewish people have suffered many calamities. The most horrible was the Holocaust *(during World War II)*. Germany, one of the most advanced and civilized nations *(supposedly a Christian nation)*, systematically murdered six million Jewish people.

Arab Moslem leaders encouraged Hitler's evil deeds and pressured British occupying forces to stop Jewish refugees from entering the Holy Land.

The British turned away boats full of refugees attempting to escape from Nazi extermination.

"...the British refused pleas by Jewish officials in early 1942 to allow the Struma, a ship carrying 769 refugees, to land in Haifa. The ship, stuck at Istanbul...was ordered by Turkish officials to sail back to it's Black Sea port of departure in Romania. The next night the ramshackle vessel sank, leaving all but one passenger dead."[1]

During World War II, the Arab Moslem leader in Jerusalem was Mufti Haj Amin al-Husseini *(cousin of PLO Chairman, Yassar Arafat)*. The Mufti supported the Nazis. He met with Hitler on November 21, 1941 as reported in his diary.

---

[1] David Dolan, *Holy War for the Promised Land*, 96.

Arab Palestinian Leader with Hitler (1941)

According to the Mufti, Hitler said to him,

"I am happy...that you are...with the Axis powers. The hour will strike when you will be the lord of the supreme word and not only the conveyer of our declarations...I am happy that you are...now in a position to add your strength to the common cause.[2]"

In 1943 the Hungarian government planned to send Jewish children to the Holy Land to escape the Nazis. In a letter the Mufti demanded that Hungary reverse the plan. The 900 children were sent to extermination camps in Poland.[3]

[2] From the personal diary of Mufti Haj Amin al-Husseini leader of the Arab Palestinians quoted by Joan Peters in *From Time Immemorial*, 436-438.

[3] Joan Peters, *From Time Immemorial*, 363, 372.

In 1943 the Mufti, Islamic leader of the Arab Palestinians, **"shed the blood of the children of Israel** at the **time of their calamity"** *(see Ezekiel 35:4-5).*

Jewish People Taken to a Death Camp

They Want Israel's Land

After World War I England occupied the Holy Land *(an area known in the west as Palestine)*. In 1917 England promised the area to the Jewish people for a homeland. In 1920 the League of Nations agreed to the creation of a homeland for the Jewish people in Palestine.

The Area Called Palestine

British-Occupied area called...
PALESTINE

Jewish Homeland

(authorized by the League of Nations 1920)

Two years after the League of Nations' mandate for a Jewish homeland, Britain gave 77% of Palestine—all of Palestine east of the Jordan River—to the Arabs, calling it Transjordan.

After the creation of the Arab Palestinian area called Transjordan in 1922, the British allowed Arabs to settle anywhere in Palestine, but Jewish people were no longer allowed to settle east of the Jordan River.

Palestine was Divided

Jews were allowed to settle **ONLY here** after 1922

TRANSJORDAN
(Arab Palestinian area)

Jews NOT ALLOWED to settle here after 1922

ARAB PALESTINIAN AREA
(authorized by the occupying British 1922)

(Note that Jewish people were allowed to settle and did settle in the mountains of Israel [the so-called West Bank] until Jordan captured the area in 1948.)

Transjordan became Jordan. Today the territory once known as Palestine is two nations, Jordan *(an Arab Palestinian State)* and Israel *(the only Jewish State).*

Palestine is Now Two Nations

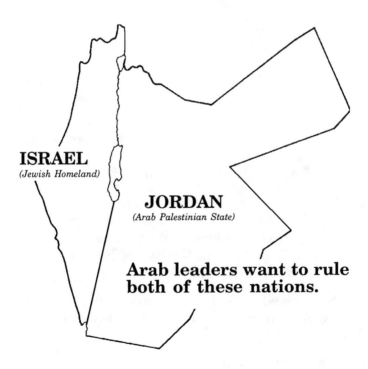

ISRAEL
(Jewish Homeland)

JORDAN
(Arab Palestinian State)

Arab leaders want to rule both of these nations.

The United Nations voted *(in 1947)* to create a Jewish state—to take effect on May 15, 1948. On the day of Israel's birth Transjordan *(now Jordan)* and five other Arab states moved to destroy the new nation of Israel by attacking them militarily on all their borders—intending to rule both Israel and Transjordan.

*"...you have said, **'These two nations and these two countries shall be mine**, and we will possess them, although the Lord was there.'"*

"'Therefore, as I live,' says the Lord God, 'I will do according to your anger and according to the envy...in your hatred against (Israel); and I will make Myself known among (Israel) when I judge you. Then you shall know that I am the Lord."
(Ezekiel 35:10-12)

Some believe that the "two nations" in verse 10 refer to Judea and Samaria. During the war, Arab forces captured Judea and Samaria, killed or drove out all the Jewish people living there, seized Jewish homes and property and annexed the two to Jordan calling them the West Bank.

The Jewish towns, villages, or kibbutzim of Atarot, Bet Haarava, Ein Tzurim, Gush Etzion, Kallia, Massuot Yizhak, Neve Yakov, Revadim and the Jewish Quarter of the Old City of Jerusalem were taken over by Jordanian forces.[1]

No Jewish people were allowed to live in Jordanian-occupied Judea and Samaria.

[1] Martin Gilbert, *The Arab-Israeli Conflict*, 47.

The Lord Protects Israel

The Bible foretells the birth of the State of Israel.

"Who has heard such a thing? Who has seen such things? Shall the earth be made to give birth in one day? Or shall a nation be born at once?...."
(Isaiah 66:8)

The earth is pregnant. A nation is to be born in one day. In verse 10 we see that that nation is Israel.

It happened as God promised. "The earth" in the form of the United Nations voted for Israel to become a nation. And on May 14th, 1948 Israel proclaimed statehood. In one day a new nation was born just as God promised.

At once the borders were opened and hundreds of thousands of Jews who survived deadly persecution in other lands entered the State of Israel—doubling the population in a few days. *("...For as soon as Zion was in labor, She gave birth to her children." [verse 8])*

When the Arabic Islamic nations around Israel attempted to destroy it at birth, they thought they were fighting only against the outnumbered and poorly armed Jewish people. They failed to recognize that **the Lord was there** *(see Ezekiel 35:10)*. To attack God's people and His Land is to attack Him. God said,

*"...I will make Myself known **among them** (Israel) when I judge you. Then you will know that I am the Lord."* *(Ezekiel 35:11)*

73

Six Arab armies and the Arab Palestinians in cooperation with the Arab League (seven nations at that time) stood like great dragons around the borders waiting for the birth of the new nation, Israel, to devour it as soon as it was born.

Only a miracle could save Israel. At that time United States Secretary of State George C. Marshall confronted a Jewish diplomat with the hopelessness of the Israeli situation,

"'...You have Arab states all around you, and your backs are to the sea. How do you expect to withstand their assault? ...I know you have some arms and your Haganah (militia), but the Arabs have regular armies. They are well trained and they have heavy arms. How can you hope to hold out?'"[1]

At Israel's birth, the wise men of the world saw no hope. But the Lord said,

"'Shall I bring to the time of birth, and not cause delivery?...shall I who cause delivery shut up the womb?' says your God. Rejoice with Jerusalem, and be glad with her....'" (Isaiah 66:9-10)

The Israeli army was outnumbered. They had little training. Their military equipment was old and unreliable. But miracles happened. Here is one example. The Arabs had prevented food from reaching the Jews of Jerusalem, but:

"In April (before the war started in May)...a weed called khubeize provided miraculous relief to the hungry (Jewish) population. The spinachlike herb

---

[1] Collins & Lapierre, *O JERUSALEM*, 359.

sprang up wild... Women scoured the fields of the city looking for it". A few weeks later an *"unseasonable three-day rain struck Jerusalem, bringing a new and totally unexpected crop of khubeiza pushing up from the soil.*

'Ah,' said (the people of Jerusalem), 'The Lord is with us. The last time when we left Egypt, He sent us manna. This time He sent us rain for the cisterns and the khubeiza.'" [2]

On the day of Israel's birth, six Arab nations attacked Israel. In a situation that seemed hopeless, Israel survived. Jordan captured most of Judea and Samaria, but the Lord saved Israel and established them as a nation. How did Israel survive? The Lord was among them just as He had promised *(see Ezekiel 35:11).* The Arab nations failed to see that they were fighting against the Lord.

Though their enemies outnumbered them, Israel survived, pushing their enemies farther back each time they were attacked.

In 1967 Arab states again prepared to attack Israel. Again the Lord fought for Israel. In six days Israel captured the West Bank, the Golan Heights, the Gaza Strip and the Sinai Peninsula. *(See the map on page 16.)* The world marveled.

The Lord was with Israel again in 1973 on Yom Kippur, when they were surprised by simultaneous attacks in the north and south. With the help of the Lord Israel fought back and won, pushing the enemies back almost to their capital cities.

[2] Collins & Lapierre, *O JERUSALEM,* 370.

Again in 1991 an Arabic Islamic leader failed to recognize that the Lord was with Israel. Iraq attacked Israel with scud missiles during the Gulf War. Thirty-nine missiles fell in Israel *(many in closely settled cities)*. Five thousand homes were destroyed, but only two people were killed as a direct result of the missiles.

Arab nations think they are fighting against only men, but in fact they are blaspheming the Lord.

THE LORD PROTECTED ISRAEL
when all these nations attacked Israel in 1948

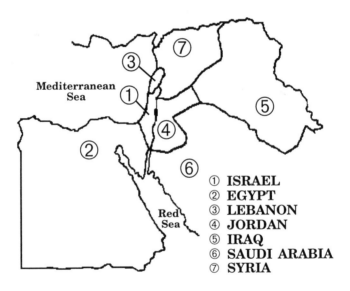

① ISRAEL
② EGYPT
③ LEBANON
④ JORDAN
⑤ IRAQ
⑥ SAUDI ARABIA
⑦ SYRIA

Ask yourself...

Could Israel have survived against all of these nations *without* God's help?

Blasphemies

"...I have heard all your blasphemies which you have spoken against the mountains of Israel, saying, 'they are desolate; they are given to us to consume.'" *(Ezekiel 35:12)*

According to His Word, the Lord set aside a Land for Himself. To demonstrate His power to the nations, He brought Israel into the Land with signs and wonders.

When Israel came from Egypt, before they entered the Land, the Lord revealed that the Children of Israel would be scattered among the nations. (Deuteronomy 31:20, 30:1-15). He said the Land would become desolate (Leviticus 26:43-45). But He promised that the desolate Land would bloom again when Israel returned (Isaiah 35:1-2). These promises were written thousands of years ago.

Later the Lord told of a time when He will bring an exodus from the north that will be greater than the exodus from Egypt. (Jeremiah 16:15, 23:8) He promised to settle the Children of Israel on the mountains of Israel.

The Lord is faithfully keeping His promises. Israel was scattered. The Land became desolate. Israel is returning. The great exodus from the north is beginning. The desert is blooming. Jewish settlements are springing up in the mountains of Israel. The truth of the Bible is proved beyond doubt.

77

In spite of all these proofs that the Bible is true, the Islamic leaders of the Arab world still refuse to accept the Word of the Lord.

Islam taught that Israel would never return to the Land. They believed that the exile of the people of Israel and the destruction of the Land was proof of the Lord's permanent rejection of the Jewish people. This contradicts the Bible *(see Leviticus 26:44-45, Jeremiah 31:35-37)*.

Israel's return brings the truth of the Koran into question. Since the day of Israel's birth, Islamic Arab forces have tried to destroy Israel. In 1948, 1956, 1967, and 1973 Islamic forces banded together to push Israel into the sea. Israel survived and captured additional land.

Only with the help of the Lord could Israel have won against such powerful enemies. Yet Islamic Arabic leaders do not accept the Lord's power and authority to set aside a Land for His special purpose.

The Lord said,

*"I have heard all your **blasphemies** which you have spoken against the mountains of Israel, saying, 'They are **desolate**; they are **given to us to consume.**"'* (*Ezekiel 35:12*)

Arab leaders thought that Judea and Samaria were **given to them to consume.** As mentioned earlier *(p. 43)* in 1948 Jewish towns and villages in Judea and Samaria *(the so-called West Bank)* were uprooted by the Arab forces of Jordan.

Everything Jewish was destroyed or taken over—homes, synagogues, businesses, hospitals and schools. Arabic forces swept away or confiscated **all** Jewish possessions. Arabic Islamic forces destroyed 34 synagogues in the Jewish Quarter of the Old City of Jerusalem.

In 1948 Arab forces took the mountains of Israel to be their possession.

"Aha! The ancient heights have become our possession."
(see Ezekiel 36:2,5)

The Lord had other plans. In 1967 Jewish people returned to the mountains of Israel, just as the Lord promised.

Note: Some say that in war both sides did the same things. But I am struck by the fact that when Arabic Islamic forces captured Judea and Samaria in 1948, Jewish places of worship were destroyed and ALL Jewish people were driven from their homes and their property was confiscated. ***No Jewish people were allowed to remain in Jordanian-occupied Judea and Samaria.***

But in 1967, when Jewish forces recaptured Judea and Samaria, hundreds of thousands of Arabic people were allowed to remain. The Dome of the Rock and other Moslem places of worship survived the war. This is a significant difference.

The PLO and Palestinians ignored the Lord's Word and His miraculous return of Israel to the Land. In 1988 they claimed the mountains of Israel as an Arabic State, naming Jerusalem as its capital. In claiming the Land given to Israel by the Lord, PLO leaders have set themselves against God.

To reject the Lord's Word is to reject the Lord. It is to call the Lord a liar. This is blasphemy! This issue is a measuring line, which determines who accepts God and who rejects Him.

They Boasted Against the Lord

The Lord said,

"You have boasted against Me...." (Ezekiel 35:13)

The Koran and the Hadith *(statements attributed to the Prophet Muhammad)* affected Arabic people's attitude toward the Jewish people.

One Hadith of the Prophet Muhammad appeared in Egyptian publications in the 1930's and 1940's.

It contained this boast,

"The resurrection of the dead will not come until the Muslims will war with the Jews and the Muslims will kill them...the trees and rocks will say, 'O Muslim, O Abdullah, here is a Jew behind me, come and kill him.'" [1]

The Lord promised to bring and is bringing Israel back to their Land. Following are quotations from Arabic leaders, who refuse to accept the Lord's authority and ability to bring the children of Israel back to the Land and to protect

---

[1] Joan Peters, *From Time Immemorial,* 73.

them. The following boast was made by the head of the Arab League on the day of Israel's birth as a nation.

"This will be a war of extermination and a momentous massacre...like the Mongolian massacres...." (Azzam Pasha, Secretary General of the Arab League, at a May 15th, 1948 press conference in Cairo as reported by the NEW YORK TIMES on May 16, 1948)

The survival of Israel in 1948 did not stop Arab boasting.

"I announce from here, on behalf of the United Arab Republic people, that this time we will exterminate Israel." (President Gamal Abdel Nasser of Egypt, speech in Alexandria, July 26, 1959)[2]

They boasted before the Six-Day war in 1967.

"The existence of Israel is an error which must be rectified. This is our opportunity to wipe out the ignominy which has been with us since 1948. Our goal is clear—to wipe Israel off the map." (President Abdel Rahman Aref of Iraq, May 31, 1967)[3]

The survival of Israel in the Six-Day war of 1967 did not stop their boasting.

"The battle with Israel must be such that, after it, Israel will cease to exist." (President Muammar Qaddafi of Libya, al-Usbu al-Arabi [Beirut] quoted by Algiers Radio, Nov. 12, 1973)[4]

---

[2] *Myths and Facts*, (Washington, DC: Near East Report, 1992), 295.
[3] Ibid., 296.
[4] Ibid.

Arabs boasted after Israel's victory in 1973.

"This racist entity in the Middle East must be destroyed and it will be destroyed one day." *(Mansour Rashid Kikhia, Libyan Ambassador to the UN, Statement to Security Council, March 24, 1976)* [5]

Palestinian leaders admit that they will use peace negotiations to destroy Israel.

"The establishment of a Palestinian state in the West Bank and Gaza will be the beginning of the downfall of the Zionist enterprise. We will be able to rely on this defeat in order to complete the struggle to realize our entire goal." *(George Habash, PLO head of PFLP June 9, 1989, "Voice of the Mountain" Radio, Lebanon)*

"...We shall pitch our tent in those places which our bullets can reach...This tent shall then form the base from which we shall later pursue the next phase." *(Farouk Kaddoumi, head of the PLO's Political Department, April 5, 1989, BBC Arabic service)*

Do the agreements that the PLO signed with Israel in 1993 and 1994 mean that they no longer intend to destroy Israel?

No. Arafat still boasts.

Arutz Sheva News Service, Wednesday, February 14, 1996

ARAFAT PREDICTS DESTRUCTION OF ISRAEL

"Yasser Arafat estimates that the final-stage agreements between the Palestinians and Israel will

---

[5] *Myths and Facts*, (Washington, DC: Near East Report, 1992), 296

ultimately bring about Israel's collapse. Arutz-7 has learned that an unpublicized meeting between Mr. Arafat and Swedish based Arab diplomats took place during Arafat's recent visit to Stockholm. Mr. Arafat's reported remarks, entitled 'The Impending Collapse of Israel,' opined that the massive import of Arabs to 'the West Bank and Jerusalem,' and the psychological warfare the Palestinians will wage against the Israelis will cause a massive emigration of Jews to the United States. "We Palestinians will takeover everything, including all of Jerusalem," Arafat declared...

"He added that the PLO plans 'to eliminate the State of Israel and establish a purely Palestinian State. We will make life unbearable for Jews...'

"In a plea for pan-Arab support, Mr. Arafat told the Arab diplomats: 'I have no use for Jews; they are and remain Jews! We now need all the help we can get from you in our battle for a united Palestine under total Arab-Muslim domination!'

"Mr. Arafat's meeting took place on January 30th, (1996) in Stockholm's Grand Hotel shortly after an official state dinner in his honor sponsored by Sweden's Foreign Minister in the hotel's 'Der Shpigal Salon'..."

Clearly the PLO has not changed. They have not forgotten their "plan of stages" *(the plan to take as much of Israel as they can by negotiations and then to drive the weakened Jewish people out of the land).* They shake hands and continue to boast that they will destroy the people they are pretending to make peace with.

The words of the PLO spokesman reveal why the PLO refuses to live in peace with Israel.

"The struggle with the Zionist enemy is not a struggle about Israel's borders, but about Israel's existence." *(Bassam Abu Sharif, a top Arafat aide and PLO spokesman, Quoted by Kuwait News Agency, May 31, 1986)[6]*

Islamic leaders continue to believe that they are fighting against—and boasting against—only men. They fail to recognize that they are opposing the Lord. The Lord reveals why they have not prevailed against Israel. The Lord says,

"You have boasted against ME and multiplied your words against ME; I have heard them...."
(Ezekiel 35:13)

Israel is Slandered

God said,

"...you (mountains of Israel) are taken up by the lips of talkers and slandered by the people...."
(Ezekiel 36:3, see also 35:12)

Slander against Israel is constant. For example a book from a well-known publishing house accuses Israeli soldiers of murdering the people of an Arab Christian village near the Sea of Galilee and burying them in a shallow mass grave. But Christians in that village told us that it did not happen.

Another published slander is that Israeli soldiers are trained to hit children on the side of the head in just the right way to make their eyes pop out. Christians who serve in the Israeli army in the disputed areas tell us this is pure slander.

God says that those who slander will bear their own shame. (See Ezekiel 36:3,7)

[6] *Myths and Facts,* (Washington, DC: Near East Report, 1992), *299.*

(Note... Please keep in mind as we continue that we are discussing sovereignty over land...not the right of individuals to live in the land. The Lord made provision in His Word for aliens to live in the Holy Land. Therefore, Arabic people may continue to live in the Land under Israeli rule.)

IS THE LORD UNFAIR ?

Some insist that Israel's possession of the Land is the cause of unrest in the Middle East. They want Israel to give the mountains of Israel, the Golan Heights and the Gaza Strip to Arab Palestinians. They think the Holy Land is Arab land.

But the Bible says that the Holy Land belongs to the Lord; and the Word of the Lord tells us that Jewish people will rule the Holy Land. Is this unfair?

Is the Lord unfair to Arabic people?

- The Lord chose Israel for a special purpose. Is this unfair to Arabic people?

- The Lord set aside a certain Land that He calls "My Land." Is this unfair?

- Shouldn't Arabic people be allowed to rule land too? Isn't it only right for them to have their own state?

- Do Jewish people rule an unfair amount of Land? How much land is ruled by Jewish people compared with Arabic-ruled lands?

ARABIC STATES

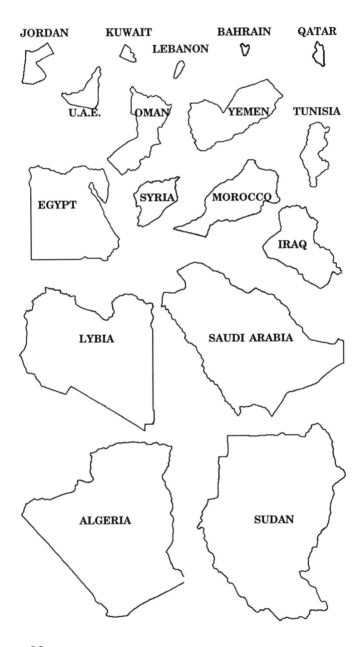

JORDAN   KUWAIT   BAHRAIN   QATAR
              LEBANON

U.A.E.   OMAN   YEMEN   TUNISIA

EGYPT   SYRIA   MOROCCO

IRAQ

LYBIA   SAUDI ARABIA

ALGERIA   SUDAN

JEWISH STATE

ISRAEL

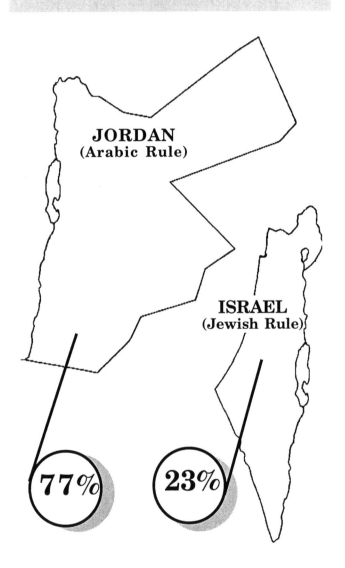

ARABS RULE
77% OF PALESTINE.

JORDAN
(Arabic Rule)

ISRAEL
(Jewish Rule)

77%

23%

What about Arab Palestinians? Has the Lord been unfair to Arab Palestinians? Shouldn't they have their own state?

The Lord is not unfair to Arab Palestinians. An Arab Palestinian state exists. 77% of Palestine is ruled by Arabic people *(the land called Jordan)*. Only 23% of Palestine is ruled by Israel. **It is shocking to look at pages 86, 87, 88 and 90 and to realize that Arabic people, who rule these lands, want Israel's land too.**

Palestinian Refugees

What about Arab Palestinian refugees? Approximately 700,000 became refugees in 1948 and 1967.

An interesting fact was uncovered by Joan Peters in her research for *From Time Immemorial*. The United Nations defines refugees as people forced to leave "permanent" or "habitual" homes. But for Arab refugees the definition was expanded to include persons who had been in "Palestine" for as little as **two years**. If only a few refugees had recently arrived, it would not have been necessary for the "two year residence" clause to be incorporated into the official United Nations refugee definition.[1]

Arabic people, who call themselves Palestinians, would have us believe that all of them had lived in "Palestine" for thousands of years. But records show that many who were designated by the UN as refugees were not natives of the area.

---

[1] Joan Peters, *From Time Immemorial*, p. 4.

COMPARISON OF ARABIC AND JEWISH
POPULATION AND LAND

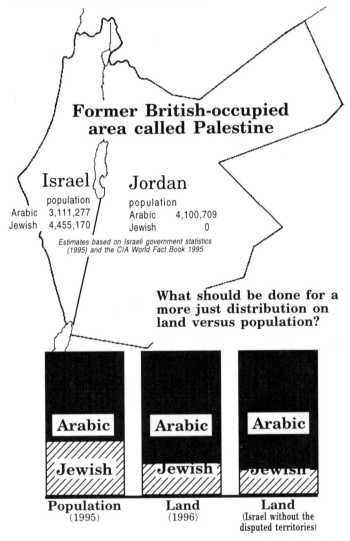

Former British-occupied area called Palestine

Israel

population

Arabic	3,111,277
Jewish	4,455,170

Jordan

population

Arabic	4,100,709
Jewish	0

Estimates based on Israeli government statistics (1995) and the CIA World Fact Book 1995

What should be done for a more just distribution on land versus population?

Arabic / Jewish — **Population** (1995)

Arabic / Jewish — **Land** (1996)

Arabic / Jewish — **Land** (Israel without the disputed territories)

In the area that once was called Palestine, Jews have less land (in proportion to population) than Arabs. Justice would suggest that more land be returned to the Jews.

Arabic refugees lived in Jordan and Egypt from 1948 to 1967 without being settled by their brothers. **Through the United Nations for 19 years the people of the world supported Arabic refugees who were living in Arabic countries.** *(In Lebanon the UN supported Arabic refugees living in an Arabic nation for 44 years.)* Arabic leaders kept the refugees in camps, for use in their propaganda war against Israel.

Jewish Refugees

From 1947 to the early 1950's **700,000 Jewish people sought refuge from Arab countries.**

"Of more than 850,000 Jews in Arab lands before Israel's statehood, fewer than 29,000 remain. Many of the Arab states...have been rendered virtually Judenrein (free of Jews—Hitler's term)"[2]

Jewish Refugees Are Settled—

In the tiny Land of Israel Jewish refugees from Arab countries—many who had to leave everything behind—are settled and are helping to settle the hundreds of thousands of immigrants from Russia, Ethiopia and other nations.

Arab Refugees Are Not Settled—

Yet with 17 nations and 500 times more land and with fabulous wealth from oil, **Arab Moslems did not settle their brothers. This is the cause of the Palestinian problem.**

---

[2] Joan Peters, *From Time Immemorial*, p. 116.

Arabic leaders refuse to settle their brothers. They deny the sovereignty of the Lord and try to destroy the people that the Lord chose for a special purpose. How can this be understood?

It can only be understood as the *ancient hatred* that the Lord condemned in Ezekiel 35:5.

Islamic Arab leaders have rebelled against the Lord—and they want western nations, the United Nations, Judaism and Christianity to rebel against Him, too. **Islamic Arabic leaders in effect are asking us to deny our faith in the truth of the Bible.**

This we cannot do!

Since the Word of the Lord is clear that Jewish people will possess and live in the so-called West Bank, he who attempts to carve a Palestinian state out of the Land set aside by God, does not know the Bible or does not fear God.

Islamic Arabic leaders...

...are asking us to deny our faith in the truth of the Bible.

HE IS LORD

Some people *(Jewish and Gentile)* think that the ingathering of Israel, which is happening today, and the new State of Israel is just a blip in history. They do not believe that this is the ingathering promised by the Lord.

Some rabbis teach that the Messiah Himself will come to set up a Jewish State. For this reason they do not believe that today's Israel is a fulfillment of God's promises.

Some ministers preach replacement theology. They believe that because Israel has sinned, the Church has replaced her—that the church will receive God's promises to Israel. This leaves Christians, who are not yet perfect, out on a limb. If God replaced Israel, what would prevent Him from replacing the not-yet-perfect Church?

Paul spoke against errors like replacement theology, when he said concerning the Jewish people,

"The gifts and the calling of God are irrevocable."
(Romans 11:29)

When God makes a promise, we can be sure that He will keep it.

Some ministers teach that Jewish people must actively seek the Lord before the prophecies of the return to the Land can be fulfilled. They point out that many Jewish people in Israel are not living holy lives and some are atheists, and therefore they insist Israel is only an accident of history.

Other Jewish and Christian leaders teach that the Jewish State and the return of Israel to the Land is proof beyond doubt of the Lord's power and faithfulness to keep His promises.

Must Jewish people be righteous, before the Lord keeps His promise to bring them home? Please look again at page 21 and look closely at the last 22 verses of chapter 36 of Ezekiel. The Lord tells us that **He will bring Israel back while they are sinful.** After they are in the Land, He will cleanse them.

"I will take you from among the nations, gather you out of all countries, and bring you into your own land. (Then) I will sprinkle clean water on you and you shall be clean...." *(Ezekiel 36:24-25)* *(See Also Jeremiah 33:7-8)*

Since millions of Jewish people have returned to the Land and miracles allowed the State of Israel to survive several wars **it is becoming increasingly difficult to argue that these things have happened by accident.**

In the last 22 verses of chapter 36 the Lord reminds us of the history of His relationship with Israel. When they were in their own Land, Israel sinned *(v. 17)*. The Lord punished them and scattered them among the nations *(v. 19)*.

The nations profaned God's name,

"When they came to the nations, wherever they went, they profaned My holy name when they said

of them, 'These are the people of the Lord, and yet they have gone out of His Land.'" (v. 20)

Because the Jewish people were exiled from their Land, the people of the nations mistakenly assumed that the Lord had rejected them forever, or that Israel's God was not strong enough to protect them. To believe that the Lord cannot or will not keep His promises is to profane God's Name—damaging His reputation and hindering those who would believe in Him.

The Lord had concern for His Holy Name *(v. 21).* He wanted everyone to know the truth about His power and faithfulness.

Therefore, He brought the Jewish people back to their Land to show His power and faithfulness. He did not bring them back because they deserved to be brought back, but for His Holy Name's sake *(v. 22 and v. 32).*

As we have said, God wants everyone to know that HE IS LORD. He is gathering Jewish people out of the nations to prove that He is Lord *(v. 23-24).*

After Israel is back in their own land, God will,

- Sprinkle clean water on them *(v. 25)*
- Give them a new heart. *(v. 26)*
- Put His Spirit in them. *(v. 27)*

We are in the midst of what the Lord describes to us in chapter 36. A Jewish State exists for the first time in more than 2,000 years. Its very existence is a miracle. The Lord is gathering Israel into the Land. They are not perfect. Some do not believe in God. The new heart for Israel is still in the future. But if the Lord is able to gather His people from the nations, who can doubt His power to pour out His Spirit upon them?

The nations do not yet know that He is Lord. He is doing great miracles in Israel, but most people do not know. They are unaware that prophecy is being fulfilled daily in Israel.

But one day the nations around Israel will realize that the Lord Himself has rebuilt the ruins and put Israel back in their Land,

*"Then the nations which are left all around you shall know that **I, the Lord, have rebuilt the ruined places** and planted what was desolate. I, the Lord, have spoken it, and **I will do it**...the ruined cities (will) be filled with flocks of men.*

Then they shall know that I am the Lord."
(Ezekiel 36:36, 38)

*Please note that Ezekiel chapter 35 (the punishment of Edom) and chapter 36 (the return to the Land) have the same purpose. Both chapters end with the same words, **"Then they shall know that I am the Lord."***

WHO WILL GIVE WARNING?

The Lord is keeping His promises because He loves all of us and wants to show us that He is faithful and that **He is the Lord of all nations.**

Moslems do not have the Bible and do not understand God's plan for Israel. They fail to see that they are opposing the Lord, and their cause is hopeless—**because no one can stop God from keeping His promises.**

Arabic people who call themselves Palestinians and Arabic nations tried to prevent the exodus of Jewish people from the former Soviet Union. They appealed to the United Nations, to Russia, to the United States and other countries to stop the movement of Jewish people from the north.

Arabic leaders have tried to prevent Jewish people from settling in the mountains of Israel—the heart of the homeland given to them by the Lord. They want the world to force Israel to give the mountains of Israel to them for a second Palestinian state.

Yet in Ezekiel the Lord tells us His plan for the mountains of Israel. Israel will return and possess them. He will multiply the Jewish people and bless them in the mountains of Israel. He warns Arab nations not to covet the Land that He has promised to Israel.

Well-meaning Christians and Jews, with an incomplete knowledge of the Bible, encourage Palestinians to claim Israel's Land. They unknowingly lead Arabic people to sin against God, and they bring themselves under condemnation by opposing the will of the Lord.

The Lord provided a map to help us through this time. This is the second time He brought large numbers of the descendants of Israel into the Holy Land. The first time they came from slavery in Egypt.

The exodus from Egypt is like a road map that shows us the meaning of events today. This road map includes the strange story of a talking donkey. Why did the Lord cause a donkey to speak?

Balaam's donkey appeals to children and tends to be one part of the Bible that everyone remembers.

Did the Lord make this story memorable for some reason? Did He plan some important event in which the lessons of this story would be vitally important?

Yes. The great exodus that is happening today is like the story of Balaam.

Balaam and the First Exodus

During the first exodus, as Israel prepared to enter the Promised Land, the tribes of Moab and Midian *(ancestors of modern Arabs—see page 51)* tried to stop them by asking a powerful man to intervene against Israel. They appealed to Balaam, a seer from Mesopotamia. *(Seers, also called prophets, were the most powerful men in that society.)*

The King of Moab wanted to stop the Children of Israel from settling in the mountains of Israel. He had a plan *(see Numbers chapters 22-24)*. He would send a delegation to hire Balaam, a man of great power, to curse Israel.

The King of Moab said to Balaam,

"...I know that he whom you bless is blessed, and he whom you curse is cursed."   *(Numbers 22:6)*

The King reasoned that, if Balaam would curse Israel, Moab might beat them in battle and drive them out of the Land. But the king did not realize that it was **the Lord** who was bringing Israel into the Holy Land. In trying to stop the return of Israel, the King of Moab was opposing the Lord.

When Balaam left his country to meet the king, the Lord's anger glowed. The Angel of the Lord with a large sword in his hand blocked Balaam's path. Balaam did not see the Angel of the Lord, but when Balaam's donkey saw Him, he walked off the path. Balaam struck the donkey.

Then the Angel of the Lord stood in a narrow place in the road with a wall on this side and a wall on that side. The donkey pushed herself against the wall, crushing Balaam's foot. Balaam struck the donkey again.

Then the Angel of the Lord stood in a narrow place with no room to pass. When the donkey saw the Angel of the Lord blocking her way, she lay down under Balaam. Balaam struck the donkey a third time.

Then the Lord opened the mouth of the donkey and she spoke.

After a brief conversation with the donkey, Balaam's eyes were opened and he saw the Angel of the Lord. The Lord warned Balaam to speak only what He told him to speak.

The tents of Israel stood in a valley in the land now called Jordan, across the river from Jericho. Three times, from three high mountains overlooking the valley, the King of Moab asked Balaam to curse Israel. And three times Balaam blessed them.

Balaam looked into the valley where the tents of Israel stood *(Numbers 24:5-6,9)* and said these words—

" *...How lovely are your tents,*
O Jacob!
Your dwellings,
O Israel!

Like valleys that stretch out,
Like gardens by the riverside,
Like aloes planted by the Lord,
Like cedars beside the waters...

Blessed is he who blesses you,
And cursed is he who curses you...."

The King of Moab wanted
Balaam to curse Israel

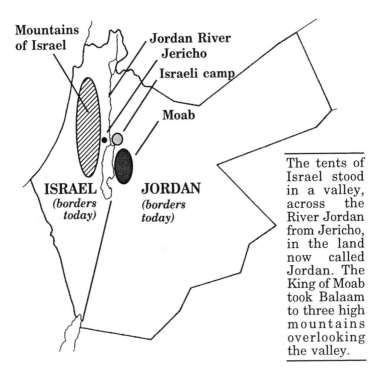

Mountains
of Israel

Jordan River

Jericho

Israeli camp

Moab

ISRAEL
(borders
today)

JORDAN
(borders
today)

The tents of Israel stood in a valley, across the River Jordan from Jericho, in the land now called Jordan. The King of Moab took Balaam to three high mountains overlooking the valley.

It is happening again

In our day Israel is returning to the Land. Like the King of Moab in the time of Balaam, leaders of the PLO and today's Arabic nations want to weaken Israel so they can drive them out of the Holy Land. These leaders believe that if they can cause the powerful men of today to turn against Israel, Israel will be forced out of the mountains of Israel.

The leaders of America and other western nations are the powerful men of today. Arabic leaders complain to powerful western leaders about Israel. They want western leaders to force Israel to stop Jewish immigration into Israel, stop Jewish settlement in the mountains of Israel and to force Israel to give the mountains of Israel *(the Land set aside by the Lord)* to the descendants of Esau, Ishmael and Moab.

The Lord promised to settle Jewish people in the mountains of Israel. Yet leaders of Arab nations insist that Jewish settlements in the mountains of Israel are the cause of unrest in the Middle East. The Lord is acting according to His Word and Arab nations are opposing Him. Will Arabic Islamic leaders succeed in deceiving Christian nations so they will oppose Him too?

Many people *(even some Jewish and Christian people)*, who are unaware of the prophecies about the West Bank, have been led into opposing God by the clever arguments of Arab Islamic leaders.

Balaam today

Leaders of America, Europe and the United Nations are like Balaam. Islamic leaders want to use them to weaken Israel.

Western leaders do not understand the consequences of opposing the return of Jewish people to the mountains of Israel. To them it is a political problem with economic rewards. Like Balaam, they do not see the Angel of the Lord in the path.

Balaam was saved from death by his donkey. Her actions made Balaam notice the Angel in his path. If western nations blunder into opposition with God, they will find that they are as helpless as Balaam before the Angel of the Lord.

They need to be warned. The donkey gave her master a bumpy ride until Balaam woke up and saw the danger. Who will give warning now?

If western political leaders are the Balaams of today, who is Balaam's donkey? Who is able to see the Angel of the Lord standing in the path? Who recognizes that the

Who is the Donkey?

Lord Himself is bringing about the return of Israel to the Holy Land?

Balaam did not have the Bible, but we do. We can know that the Lord has ordained Jewish settlement in the West Bank. Those who believe the Bible can give warning *(like Balaam's donkey)* to the leaders of western nations. They can speak out to warn the Balaams of today about the danger ahead.

Will western leaders listen to Balaam's donkey? Western leaders ride on public opinion. Like a man riding on a donkey in the desert, western leaders cannot survive for long if they ignore public opinion. Millions of Jewish and Christian voices raised together could make leaders see the Angel of the Lord in the path.

Arabic People need to be warned too

Most Arabic people do not have the Bible. They do not know that to oppose Jewish resettlement of the Holy Land is to oppose the will of the Lord. They cannot see that they are setting themselves against the Lord. Most of them are unaware of the words of Ezekiel chapter 35 warning them of the consequences of trying to destroy Israel.

What can **YOU** do?

DO NOT... encourage Arabic people to oppose the will of the Lord. Arabic people do not know the great danger they are in. They need to be told of God's love for them—that the Lord is doing these things to show all people that He is their Lord.

As you have seen in this book the Lord has blessed the Arabic people with 500 times more land than Israel. He blessed Arabic nations with fabulous wealth in oil. The Lord has not been unfair or unjust to them. He has blessed them. And yet they insist upon trying to take away the tiny Land of Israel. Do not be misled by their attempts to make you curse Israel.

DO... Tell all your friends what you have learned and encourage them to read this book.

Many Jewish and Christian people are unaware of the facts you have just read. Encourage your rabbi or pastor and the members of your congregation to read this book. Show them what the Bible says.

Tell them that the Lord is not unfair. Through the weakness of Israel, the Lord is demonstrating His great power and Lordship. He is doing these things for the benefit of everyone in the world—including Palestinians—to let them know that He and only He is Lord. Encourage them to speak out for Israel.

Nations that oppose the Lord are in danger. If the leaders of your nation are going against the Word of the Lord concerning Israel, they are exposing **YOU** to danger. Like Balaam's donkey, walk off the path. Refuse to go forward. Speak out until they wake up and understand that the Angel of the Lord is standing in their path.

As Balaam said, those who bless Israel will be blessed, and those who curse Israel will be cursed.

If you see an Angel in the path...

EZEKIEL CHAPTERS 35 AND 36
(New King James Version)

1 Moreover the word of the Lord came to me, saying...

2 "Son of man, **set your face against Mount Seir and prophesy against it,**

3 "And say to it, 'Thus says the Lord God...

"Behold, O Mount Seir, I am against you; and I will stretch out My hand against you, and make you most desolate;

4 I shall lay your cities waste, and you shall be desolate. Then you shall know that I am the LORD.

5 "Because you have had an ancient hatred, and have shed the blood of the children of Israel by the power of the sword at the time of their calamity, when their iniquity came to an end,

6 "therefore, as I live," says the Lord God, "I will prepare you for blood, and blood shall pursue you; since you have not hated blood, therefore blood shall pursue you.

7 "Thus I will make Mount Seir most desolate, and cut off from it the one who leaves and the one who returns.

8 "And I will fill its mountains with the slain; on your hills and in your valleys and in all your ravines those who are slain by the sword shall fall.

9 "I will make you perpetually desolate, and your cities shall be uninhabited; then you shall know that I am the LORD.

10 "Because you have said, 'These two nations and these two countries shall be mine, and we will possess them,' although the LORD was there,

Appendix

11 "therefore, as I live," says the Lord God, "I will do according to your anger and according to your envy which you showed in your hatred against them; and I will make Myself known among them when I judge you.

12 "Then you shall know that I am the LORD. I have heard all your blasphemies which you have spoken against the mountains of Israel, saying, 'They are desolate; they are given to us to consume.'

13 "Thus with your mouth you have boasted against Me and multiplied your words against Me; I have heard them."

14 'Thus says the Lord God...

"The whole earth will rejoice when I make you desolate.

15 "As you rejoiced because the inheritance of the house of Israel was desolate, so I will do to you; you shall be desolate, O Mount Seir, as well as all of Edom—all of it! **Then they shall know that I am the LORD.**"'

CHAPTER 36

1 "And you, son of man, **prophesy to the mountains of Israel**, and say, 'O mountains of Israel, hear the word of the LORD!

2 Thus says the Lord God...

"Because the enemy has said of you, 'Aha! The ancient heights have become our possession,'"

3 "therefore prophesy, and say, 'Thus says the Lord God...

"Because they made you desolate and swallowed you up on every side, so that you became the possession of the rest of the nations, and you are taken up by the lips of talkers and slandered by the people"—

4 'therefore, O mountains of Israel, hear the word of the Lord God! Thus says the Lord God to the mountains, the hills, the rivers, the valleys, the desolate wastes, and the cities that have been forsaken, which became plunder and mockery to the rest of the nations all around

5 'therefore thus says the Lord God...

"Surely I have spoken in My burning jealousy against the rest of the nations and against all Edom, who gave My land to themselves as a possession, with wholehearted joy and spiteful minds, in order to plunder its open country.

6 "Therefore prophesy concerning the land of Israel, and say to the mountains, the hills, the rivers, and the valleys, 'Thus says the Lord God:

"Behold, I have spoken in My jealousy and My fury, because you have borne the shame of the nations."

Appendix

7 'Therefore thus says the Lord God...

"I have raised My hand in an oath that surely the nations that are around you shall bear their own shame.

8 "But you, O mountains of Israel, you shall shoot forth your branches and yield your fruit to My people Israel, for they are about to come.

9 "For indeed I am for you, and I will turn to you, and you shall be tilled and sown.

10 "I will multiply men upon you, all the house of Israel, all of it; and the cities shall be inhabited and the ruins rebuilt.

11 "I will multiply upon you man and beast; and they shall increase and bear young; I will make you inhabited as in former times, and do better for you than at your beginnings. Then you shall know that I am the LORD.

12 "Yes, I will cause men to walk on you, My people Israel; they shall take possession of you, and you shall be their inheritance; no more shall you bereave them of children.'

13 'Thus says the Lord God...

"Because they say to you, 'You devour men and bereave your nation of children,'"

14 "therefore you shall devour men no more, nor bereave your nation anymore," says the Lord God.

15 "Nor will I let you hear the taunts of the nations anymore, nor bear the reproach of the peoples anymore, nor shall you cause your nation to stumble anymore," says the Lord God.'"

16 Moreover the word of the LORD came to me, saying:

17 "Son of man, when the house of Israel dwelt in their own land, they defiled it by their own ways and deeds; to Me their way was like the uncleanness of a woman in her customary impurity.

18 "Therefore I poured out My fury on them for the blood they had shed on the land, and for their idols with which they had defiled it.

19 "So I scattered them among the nations, and they were dispersed throughout the countries; I judged them according to their ways and their deeds.

20 "When they came to the nations, wherever they went, they profaned My holy name—when they said of them...

'These are the people of the LORD, and yet they have gone out of His land.'

21 "But I had concern for My holy name, which the house of Israel had profaned among the nations wherever they went.

22 "Therefore say to the house of Israel, 'Thus says the Lord God...

"I do not do this for your sake, O house of Israel, but for My holy name's sake, which you have profaned among the nations wherever you went.

23 "And I will sanctify My great name, which has been profaned among the nations, which you have profaned in their midst; and the nations shall know that I am the LORD," says the Lord God, "when I am hallowed in you before their eyes.

24 "For I will take you from among the nations, gather you out of all countries, and bring you into your own land.

25 "Then I will sprinkle clean water on you, and you shall be clean; I will cleanse you from all your filthiness and from all your idols.

Appendix

26 "I will give you a new heart and put a new spirit within you. I will take the heart of stone out of your flesh and give you a heart of flesh.

27 "I will put My Spirit within you and cause you to walk in My statutes, and you will keep My judgments and do them.

28 "Then you shall dwell in the land that I gave to your fathers; you shall be My people, and I will be your God.

29 "I will deliver you from all your uncleannesses. I will call for the grain and multiply it, and bring no famine upon you.

30 "And I will multiply the fruit of your trees and the increase of your fields, so that you need never again bear the reproach of famine among the nations.

31 "Then you will remember your evil ways and your deeds that were not good; and you will loathe yourselves in your own sight, for your iniquities and your abominations.

32 "Not for your sake do I do this," says the Lord God, "let it be known to you. Be ashamed and confounded for your own ways, O house of Israel!"

33 Thus says the Lord God...

"On the day that I cleanse you from all your iniquities, I will also enable you to dwell in the cities, and the ruins shall be rebuilt.

34 "The desolate land shall be tilled instead of lying desolate in the sight of all who pass.

35 "So they will say, 'This land that was desolate has become like the garden of Eden; and the wasted, desolate and ruined cities are now fortified and inhabited.'

36 "Then the nations which are left all around you shall know that I, the LORD, have rebuilt the ruined places and planted what was desolate. I, the LORD, have spoken it, and I will do it."

37 'Thus says the Lord God...

"I will also let the house of Israel inquire of Me to do this for them: I will increase their men like a flock.

38 "Like a flock offered as holy sacrifices like the flock at Jerusalem on its feast days, so shall the ruined cities be filled with flocks of men. **Then they shall know that I am the LORD.""**

Bibliography

Alroy, Gil Carl. *Behind the Middle East Conflict, The Real Impasse Between Arab and Jew.* New York, 1975.

Avneri, Arieh. *The Claim of Dispossession: Jewish Land Settlement and the Arabs, 1878—1948.* Herzl Press, New York, 1982.

Bachi, Roberto. *The Population of Israel.* Jerusalem, 1974.

Bennett, Ramon. *Philistine: The Great Deception.* Arm of Salvation, Jerusalem, 1995.

_____. *When Day and Night Cease* (2nd ed.). Arm of Salvation, Jerusalem, 1993.

_____. *Saga: Israel and the Demise of Nations.* Arm of Salvation, Jerusalem, 1993.

Bernadotte, Folke. *To Jerusalem.* London, 1951.

Bethman, Erich W. *Decisive Years in Palestine 1918-48.* New York 1957.

Bible, The New King James Version. Thomas Nelson Publishers, New York.

Buckingham, J.S. *Travels in Palestine.* London, 1821.

De Haas, Jacob. *History of Palestine, the Last Two Thousand Years.* New York, 1934.

De Lamartine, Alphonse. *A Pilgrimage to the Holy Land.* Trans. from French. New York. 1948.

Dixon, Murray. *Whose Promised Land? Conflict in Palestine—Israel.* Heinemann History Project. Octopus, Auckland, 1991.

Dodd, Peter, and Barakat, Halim. *River Without Bridges: A study of the Exodus of the 1967 Arab Palestinian refugees.* Insisute for Palestine Studies, Beirut, 1969.

Dolan, David. *Holy War for the Promised Land.* Hodder & Stoughton, London, 1991.

Dupuy, Trevor, N. *Elusive Victory: The Arab Israeli Wars 1947-1974.* Harper & Row Publishers, New York, 1978.

Encyclopedia Judaica. Eds. C. Roth., G. Wigoder. Jerusalem, 1972.

Evans, Mike. *Israel—America's key to survival.* Logos International, Plainfield, 1981.

Gilbert, Martin. *The Arab-Israeli Conflict...Its History in Maps.* Weidenfeld & Nicolson, London, 1979.

Granott, A. *The Land System in Palestine, History and Structure.* London, 1952.

Grant, George. *The Blood of the Moon.* Wolgemuth & Hyatt, Brentwood, 1991.

Granovsky, A. *Land and the Jewish Reconstruction of Palestine.* Jerusalem, 1931.

Gur, Lt. General Mordechai. *The Battle for Jerusalem* (Original Hebrew title: Har Habayit Beyadeinu). Steimatzky, Israel, 1974.

Gurevich, David, and Gertz, Aaron. *Jewish Agricultural Settlement in Israel.* Jerusalem, 1938.

Hedding, Malcolm. *Understanding Israel.* Sovergn World, England, 1989.

Hull, William L. *The Fall and Rise of Israel: The story of the Jewish people during the time of their dispersal and regathering.* Zondervan, Grand Rapids, 1954.

Herzog, Chaim. *The Arab-Israeli Wars.* Arms & Armour Press, Lionel Leventhal Ltd., London, 1982.

Huntington, Ellsworth. *Palestine and its Transformation.* Boston, 1911.

Jones, Phillip. *Britain and Palestine 1914-1948.* Oxford, 1979.

Bibliography

Josephus, Flavious. *The Complete Works of Flavius Josephus, the Celebrated Jewish Historian.* Trans. W. Whiston. Philadelphia, 1895.

Katz, Samuel M. *Battleground: Facts and Fantasy in Palestine.* Bantam, New York, 1973.

_____. Guards *Without Frontiers: Israel' War Against Terrorism.* Arms and Armour, London, 1990.

_____. *Israel Versus Jibril: The Thirty-Year War Against a Master Terrorist.* Paragon House, New York, 1993.

_____. *Follow Me! A History of Israel's Military Elite.* Arms & Armour Press, London, 1988.

Kimche, David, and Brawly, Dan. *The Sand-Storm. The Arab-Israeli War of 1967: Prelude and Aftermath.* Stein & Day Publishers, New York, 1968.

Kunnas, Unto. *Kaarlo Syvanto--Pioneer...Forty years in Israel* (original in Finnish, from translation by Paul and Hilja Karvonen, 1987).

Lewis, Bernard. *The Arabs in History,* 4th rev. ed. Harper-Colophon Books, New York, 1966.

Liebler, Isi. *The Case for Israel.* The Globe Press, Australia, 1972.

Mandel, Neville. *Arabs and Zionism Before World War I.* Berkeley, 1976.

Manning, Reverend Samuel. *Those Holy Fields.* London, 1874.

Mossek, M. *Palestine Immigration Policy Under Sir Herbert Samuel.* London, 1978.

Myths and Facts 1992. Washington, DC: Near East Report.

Parkes, James William. *A History of Palestine from 135 A.D. to Modern Times.* New York, 1949.

Pearlman, Maurice. *Mufti of Jerusalem.* London, 1947.

Peters, Joan. *From Time Immemorial,* Joan Peters. Harper & Row, New York, 1984.

Pinner, Walter. *How Many Arab Refugees?* London, 1959.

Rabinovich, Abraham. *The Greening of a Wasteland, The Jerusalem Post Magazine* p. 8, March 27, 1992, The Jerusalem Post, Jerusalem, 1992.

Roumani, Maurice. *The Case of the Jews from Arab Countries: A Neglected Issue.* Jerusalem, 1975.

Sachar, Howard M. *A History of Israel: From the Rise of Zionism to Our Time.* Alfred A Knoff, New York, 1991.

Schechtman, Joseph B. *The Arab Refugee Problem.* New York, 1952.

_____. *On Wings of Eagles, The Plight, Exodus and Homecoming of Oriental Jewry.* New York, 1961.

Shorrosh, Anis A. *Islam Revealed: A Christian Arab's View of Islam.* Thomas Nelson, Nashville, 1988.

Smith, George Adam. *The Historical Geography of the Holy Land.* London, 1931.

Stillman, Norman A. *The Jews of Arab Lands: A History and Source Book.* Philadelphia, 1979.

Stoyanovsky, J. *The Mandate for Palestine.* London, New York, Toronto, 1928.

Thomson, William M. *The Land and the Book.* London, 1873.

Tristram, H. B. *The Land of Israel: A Journal of Travels in Palestine.* London, 1865.

Twain, Mark. *The Innocents Abroad.* Literary Classics of the United States, New York, 1984.

Biblical and Year Index

116

Index

Index

118

Index

Index